Cookie Craft

From Baking to Luster Dust

Cookie Craft

Designs and Techniques for Creative Cookie Occasions

Valerie
Peterson
& Janice
Fryer

FALL RIVER PRESS

© 2007 by Valerie Peterson and Janice Fryer

This 2011 edition published by Fall River Press,
by arrangement with Storey Publishing

Photography © by Ellie Miller Photo
Food styling by Sara Neumeier
Prop styling by Karen Quatsoe
Color illustrations © by Sophie Blackall
Black-and-white illustrations by Alison Kolesar

Edited by Margaret Sutherland and Elaine M. Cissi
Art direction by Alethea Morrison
Text production by Jennifer Jepson Smith

Fall River Press
122 Fifth Avenue
New York, NY 10011

ISBN: 978-1-4351-2945-0

Printed and bound in China

1 3 5 7 9 10 8 6 4 2

To our moms,
Rowena and Mildred,
for teaching us the craft . . .

And to our dads,
Robert and Gordon,
who were always willing to eat our efforts!

ACKNOWLEDGMENTS

Our thanks to Pam Art for warmly welcoming us to her house, and to Walter Wentz for making the auspicious introduction. We're grateful to Margaret Sutherland, a very smart cookie, for pulling us in and pulling it all together; and to Deborah Balmuth for her always-calm support.

The concept of *Cookie Craft* was brilliantly illuminated by Alethea Morrison and her creative team, including Ellie Miller, Sophie Blackhall, Alison Kolesar, and the exceptionally talented and persevering Sara Neumeier. Our thanks to all.

We are indebted to the many, many behind-the-scenes people whose hands helped take the book from proposal to bookseller and beyond. Special shout-outs to Elaine Cissi, Elinor Goodwin, Stephanie Long and her team, Wes Seeley, and the members of the Storey and Workman sales forces, who welcomed this book with great enthusiasm — we don't *think* it was just because we brought cookies!

Our deepest appreciation to our agent, Jennifer Griffin, for easing our transition to "the other side," and for always helping us to see the big cookie when we were only looking at the crumbs.

To our especially tireless advisors—"Sascha's mom," Scott Dare, and Liz Harwell — a thousand thanks for your time and palates. To our creative guinea pigs, Sarah Durand, Sharon Gamboa, the McGowan family — especially Jane, Henry, Patrick, Madeleine, Charlotte, and John — Gemma Nedelec, Keith Pfeffer, and Mary Beth Thomas: our gratitude for your willingness and, always, for your good humor.

We are fortunate to have family, friends, and colleagues who made available their wisdom, advice, hands, shoulders, and taste buds. Thanks especially to Nanci Andersen, Rose Arlia, Steve Atinsky, the Bauers, Sandy Bell, the Bogdanovics, Rachel Bressler, Sandra Carey, Diana Cisek, Linda Dickey, Mary Dunn, the Finns, the Firstenbergs, Debbie Fryer, Jennifer Fryer, Mildred Fryer, Marge Ginsburg, the entire gang at ICE, Virginia Jenkins, David Latt (whose cookbook *we're* waiting for), Emily Loose, the Lyngholms, Maryann Manelski, Leigh Marchant, the McSpedons, Sydney Miner, Eileen O'Neill, the extended Peterson family — especially Beverly, Lisa, Robert, and Rowena — Julia Pinto, Carolyn Rostkowski, the Tedeschis, the Tonons, the Towers, Paul and Lisa Von Drasek, and Diane Weingarten. For the innumerable others who have expressed their unflagging and enthusiastic support, please know how much we appreciate it.

Valerie would like to acknowledge the many colleagues and authors with whom she's worked, and from whom she's learned — especially her first "cookies," Kevin Morrissey and the late Barry Bluestein. Her unwavering thanks go out to Janice, whose energy, quest for knowledge, and baker's soul made this book possible.

Janice would like to thank Karen Daley, who started her on this journey; and Valerie, whose creative mind is truly amazing. Without her, this book would still be just a great idea.

CONTENTS

PREFACE

Thanks to our moms, Mildred Fryer and Rowena "Weenie" Peterson, we each have always been comfortable in the kitchen. Janice has memories of baking under Mildred's tutelage and to this day remembers the first lesson she learned: Baking is an exact science and measurements must be precise. This was frustrating to young Janice when it came time to lick the beaters because Mildred would scrape every last bit of batter from them for fear the recipe wouldn't turn out right if she didn't. Although Mildred and Weenie both made plenty of cookies in their day, neither had much time for royal icing, so we each looked elsewhere for that part of our cookie education.

As friends and colleagues with a common interest in baking, we coincidentally realized one holiday season that we were looking for the same thing: a cookie decorating book to instruct and inspire us. We didn't find exactly what we envisioned, but we happily shared information and resources with each other and were able to take our cookie decorating to the next level. From making delicious, uniform sugar cookies that don't spread during baking to designing cookie decorations and preparing the ever-temperamental royal icing, we came by our knowledge with plenty of research and perfected our techniques with our own trial and error.

As we became confident in our cookie decorating, we found ourselves stretching the boundaries of what we'd learned and exploring techniques we hadn't seen anywhere to indulge our inner artists—for example, imprinting designs on cookies before baking to make a simple cat's face, or layering unbaked cookies to create a Thanksgiving turkey, or even building cookie structures to hold more cookies, like our Santa's sleigh centerpiece. Sometimes we felt more like crafters than bakers, but the results of our efforts are as delicious to eat as they are beautiful or fun to look at.

Over the years, as we were learning a lot the hard way, we kept saying, "Someone should write a book." One day we looked at each other and realized we could be the "someones." We hope you find what you need in *Cookie Craft* — a design to inspire you, a time saving tip, a new technique, a favorite cookie recipe, or even just the encouragement to create something delicious and beautiful, and to have fun doing it.

Here's the thing . . .   *In cookies as in life . . .*

it's all about the journey. We'll be with you along the way.

Janice & Valerie

cookie craft inspirations

Welcome to *Cookie Craft!* Part baking, part artful expression, cookie crafting allows you to create treats that are as delightful to the eye as they are to the taste buds. You may be a cookie beginner, or you may have years of decorating behind you. Our goal is to give you all the information you need to take your cookie crafting to the next level — whatever level that may be. We'll share our hard-won hints and tips so you can maximize your cookie-making enjoyment and minimize wasted energy. We've broken down the various steps as thoroughly as possible for those of you who've never decorated before. But once you get started, you'll see it's easier than it seems — *then* it becomes addictive.

But where to start? Here's what you'll find as you work your way through the book. We always start with a delicious cookie — and the best cookies for decorating are flat on top, to create a uniform decorating surface. Using our recipes and our *roll-chill-cut method* with cookie slats (page 83) ensures that every cookie you bake will be the same thickness and speeds the baking process.

The cookies shown here are ideas
to inspire you. You're the creative genius –
we're just here to nudge you along!

If you're a beginning cookie crafter, you may want to start with decorating your *unbaked* cookies. There are a variety of easy prebaking decorating techniques (outlined in chapter 5), such as affixing cookie add-ons (such as the nuts on the Thanksgiving turkeys) or imprinting cookies (as on some of the acorns). Because most of these techniques don't require special equipment, it's a good place for you to get your decorating feet wet.

In the realm of cookie crafting, decorating with royal icing can be a tremendous amount of fun — think of the cookie as your canvas and your icing colors as your paint (wearing a beret is optional). It does take a little practice, but you can get some experience with simple designs even before you buy any special decorating equipment by using just a zip-top freezer bag (as we did with the snowflakes and some of the fall leaves).

Maybe you're a confident baker who's handy in the kitchen; maybe you've even amassed a collection of cookie cutters but have never been motivated to use them beyond cutting out shapes and sprinkling them with some colored sugar. If so, you're much like we were when we first started decorating. There's a bit to learn — but you'll have a great time unleashing your inner cookie crafter. You'll want to master the royal icing piping and flooding techniques (that is, outlining and filling the cookies with royal icing). You can practice your piping skills with the template on page 105, and then you're ready to explore the wealth of royal icing techniques pictured on cookies throughout the book.

If you're already an accomplished decorator, we hope to provide you with a few hints you haven't thought of or ideas to inspire you, especially with the showstoppers in chapter 7 (see page 121).

For all levels, the extensive photo arrays that follow provide more than two hundred designs for you to copy or use for inspiration in your own decorated cookie planning. Let your cookie cutters' boundaries inspire you! A six-pointed Star of David can become a sheriff's badge for a birthday boy's party. A gingerbread man can become an astronaut. Round cookie cutters can make everything from a spiderweb to a baby's bib. Look at your cookie cutters with an open mind — what can you create? For sharing your cookie crafting, we tell you how to pack and ship your cookies and how to orchestrate parties, swaps, and bake sales (see chapters 8 and 9).

So now you're ready to begin. And if you have any hesitation, we'll give you this food for thought: In cookies as in life, we learn from our mistakes. In *Cookie Craft* the lessons will be sweet, because you get to eat your mistakes — they're pretty tasty!

HERE'S THE THING
ABOUT COOKIE CRAFT METHODS

Everyone has his or her favorite way of doing things. Once you've had some cookie baking and decorating practice, our ways might not be yours. We're fine with that – and if you come up with a better shortcut, let us know. But here we hope we'll get you started in the right direction and in the right spirit to have fun with your cookies.

cookie craft for holidays and seasons

Holidays are the times to keep traditions and make new ones. Cookie making has long been a beloved activity, shared by parents and children, friends and neighbors. While short-cuts sometimes seem efficient, there is no substitute for a home-baked cookie made with fresh ingredients. Iconic holiday shapes, such as Valentine's Day hearts, Halloween pumpkins, and Christmas ornaments, lend themselves to a wide variety of decorating possibilities. Cookie craft time can be family together time — many beloved memories are made and kept in the kitchen.

NEW YEAR'S

Usher in "the new" with sweet celebrations! (Maybe a last hurrah before the diet resolutions kick in?) In addition to the cookies pictured here, number-shaped cookies can proclaim the date on the new calendar. Some traditional New Year's cookie-cutter shapes can double for other milestones — for example, champagne glasses for wedding congratulations and party hats for birthdays.

cookies featured

1 *Champagne glass;* **2** *White champagne glass;* **3** *Striped noisemaker;* **4** *Nearly midnight clock;* **5** *Champagne bottle;* **6** *Striped party hat;* **7** *Polka-dot party hat;* **8** *Times Square ball;* **9** *Polka-dot noisemaker;* **10** *Striped party hat*

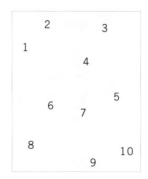

decorating instructions

1 **CHAMPAGNE GLASS** Pipe and flood "champagne"; sugar on wet flood. Affix gold dragees with piping icing on dry sugar.

2 **WHITE CHAMPAGNE GLASS** *Layer 1:* Pipe and flood glass; let dry. *Layer 2:* Pipe and flood "champagne"; sugar on wet flood.

3 **STRIPED NOISEMAKER** *Prebaking:* Use candy cane cookie cutter. *After baking:* Pipe and flood body; flood stripes on wet flood. Paint mouthpiece and band with luster dust on dry flood; pipe "noise."

4 **NEARLY MIDNIGHT CLOCK** Pipe and flood circle; add concentric circles with wet on wet flood. Pipe hands and numbers on dry flood; affix dragee with piping icing on dry flood.

5 **CHAMPAGNE BOTTLE** *Layer 1:* Pipe and flood neck, cork, and label; let dry. *Layer 2:* Paint neck, cork, and label design with luster dust; pipe outline detail on label;

let dry to touch. Paint plain portions of bottle with corn syrup; sprinkle with sanding sugar. In addition, we like to write in the actual new year with a food-safe marking pen.

6 **STRIPED PARTY HAT** Pipe and flood triangle; flood stripes on wet flood; drop dragee on wet flood.

7 **POLKA-DOT PARTY HAT** Pipe and flood triangle; flood dots on wet flood. Pipe pom-pom and edge accents on dry flood.

8 **TIMES SQUARE BALL** Pipe and flood circle; paint luster dust on dry flood. Affix dragees with piping icing on dry luster dust. For a quicker cookie, skip the luster dust and drop the dragees right onto the wet flood.

9 **POLKA-DOT NOISEMAKER** *Prebaking:* Use candy cane cookie cutter. *After baking:* Pipe and flood body; flood polka dots on wet flood; pipe "noise."

10 **STRIPED PARTY HAT** See cookie 6.

WINTER

Snow day? When it's time to come in from the cold, cookie baking and decorating can provide hours of indoor fun for kids and adults alike. It doesn't have to be complicated — for super-simple snowflakes, round, dark (chocolate or gingerbread) cookies can be piped with white icing using just a zip-top bag.

cookies featured

1 *Blue-scarfed snowman;* **2** *Round snowflake;* **3** *Blue snowflake;* **4** *Silver snowflake;* **5** *Blue hat with white jimmies;* **6** *Cutout snowflake;* **7** *Pretzel-armed snowman;* **8** *Ice skate;* **9** *Three-dot mitten;* **10** *Polka-dot mitten;* **11** *Three-dot hat;* **12** *Dotted snowflake*

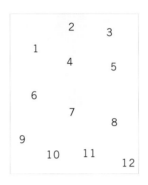

decorating instructions

1 **BLUE-SCARFED SNOWMAN** *Layer 1:* Pipe and flood body; let dry. *Layer 2:* Pipe and flood hat and scarf; sugar on wet flood. Pipe eyes and mouth on dry flood.

2 **ROUND SNOWFLAKE** Pipe lines and dots; sugar on wet piping. Try this one with a zip-top bag.

3 **BLUE SNOWFLAKE** Pipe and flood; flood snowflake lines with wet flood. For a more precise effect, do the lines with piping on wet flood.

4 **SILVER SNOWFLAKE** *Layer 1:* Pipe and flood; let dry. *Layer 2:* Paint luster dust on dry icing; pipe lines on dry luster dust; sugar on wet piped icing. For a quicker cookie, omit layer one, and instead paint entire cookie with luster dust; proceed with icing.

5 **BLUE HAT WITH WHITE JIMMIES** Pipe and flood body of hat; let dry to the touch. Pipe and flood band and pom-pom; sprinkle wet flood with jimmies. Pipe stripes.

6 **CUTOUT SNOWFLAKE** Pipe outlines and snowflake tips; sugar on wet piping. Pipe dots after sugaring.

7 **PRETZEL-ARMED SNOWMAN** *Layer 1:* Pipe, flood, and sugar hat. Pipe and flood body; let dry completely. *Layer 2:* Pipe mouth and nose. Affix candy eyes and pretzel arms with piping icing.

8 **ICE SKATE** *Layer 1:* Pipe and flood entire skate; let dry. *Layer 2:* Paint luster dust on skate blade; let dry. Pipe outline and laces.

9 **THREE-DOT MITTEN** *Layer 1:* Pipe and flood entire mitten; let dry. *Layer 2:* Pipe dots using small round pastry tip; pipe band using larger round pastry tip.

10 **POLKA-DOT MITTEN** *Layer 1:* Pipe and flood entire mitten. Flood polka dots on wet flood. *Layer 2:* Pipe and flood band; sugar on wet flood.

11 **THREE-DOT HAT** *Layer 1:* Pipe and flood entire hat; let dry. *Layer 2:* Pipe dots using small round pastry tip; pipe pom-pom and band using larger round pastry tip.

12 **DOTTED SNOWFLAKE** Pipe details; sugar on wet piping.

cookie craft inspirations

VALENTINE'S DAY

Nothing says "I love you" like handmade cookies — especially if they're beautifully decorated. Like love, heart cutters come in many variations, and the resulting cookies will certainly be the way to anyone's affections.

cookies featured

1 *Pink heart with cutout;* **2** *White heart with grid;*
3 *Red heart with heart stripes;* **4** *Chocolate and pink heart with small cookie heart;* **5** *Pink heart with grid;*
6 *Chocolate heart with jimmies;* **7** *Sugared heart;*
8 *Red heart with cutout;* **9** *Hugs and kisses;* **10** *Small red heart;* **11** *Chocolate herringbone heart;* **12** *Pink herringbone heart*

```
  1      2        3
          5        6
  4
          8        9
  7
  10    11        12
```

decorating instructions

1 **PINK HEART WITH CUTOUT** *Prebaking:* Cut out center heart. *After baking, layer 1:* Pipe and flood; let dry. *Layer 2:* Pipe dots; pipe and flood white heart; sugar wet piping and flood.

2 **WHITE HEART WITH GRID** *Layer 1:* Pipe and flood entire heart; let dry. *Layer 2:* Pipe pink grid lines; pipe red grid lines over pink. Pipe dots at grid intersections.

3 **RED HEART WITH HEART STRIPES** Pipe and flood entire heart; apply wet flood dots in alternating colors in rows; draw a toothpick from top to bottom of row, through the centers of the dots, to create hearts.

4 **CHOCOLATE AND PINK HEART WITH SMALL COOKIE HEART** *Layer 1:* Pipe and flood heart within the heart; let dry. *Layer 2:* Pipe dot border around dried flood; affix smaller cutout cookie with piping icing.

5 **PINK HEART WITH GRID** *Layer 1:* Pipe and flood; let dry. *Layer 2:* Pipe grid and outline; affix dragees to wet piping at grid intersections.

6 **CHOCOLATE HEART WITH JIMMIES** Pipe and flood white heart; sprinkle jimmies on wet flood. Pipe dots.

7 **SUGARED HEART** Pipe and flood; sugar on wet flood.

8 **RED HEART WITH CUTOUT** *Prebaking:* Cut out small heart in center of cookie. *After baking:* Pipe and flood; let dry. Pipe dots on dry flood.

9 **HUGS AND KISSES** Pipe and flood. Flood dots on wet flood. For hearts, draw toothpick through dots.

10 **SMALL RED HEART** Pipe and flood.

11 **CHOCOLATE HERRINGBONE HEART** *Layer 1:* Pipe and flood pink heart. Flood horizontal red stripes on wet flood; draw toothpick vertically through wet stripe, alternating direction from top to bottom, bottom to top; let dry. *Layer 2:* Pipe dots around border of flood and of cookie.

12 **PINK HERRINGBONE HEART** *Layer 1:* Pipe and flood. Flood horizontal stripes on wet flood; draw toothpick vertically through wet stripe, alternating direction from top to bottom, bottom to top; let dry. *Layer 2:* Pipe dots.

WINTER INTO SPRING

It's not yet warm enough to come out of hibernation, but you're longing for flowers and greenery. Why not use your snowflake cookie cutters and span the seasons with images that evoke both?

cookies featured

1 *Sparkling dotted flower;* **2** *Yellow outline flower;*
3 *Blue and yellow flower;* **4** *Blue filigree flower;*
5 *Sparkling dotted flower;* **6** *Sparkling blue flower;*
7 *Blue and yellow outline flower;* **8** *Sparkling yellow flower;* **9** *Plaid flower;* **10** *Blue flower*

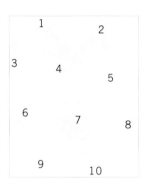

decorating instructions

1 **SPARKLING DOTTED FLOWER** *Layer 1:* Pipe and flood; let dry. *Layer 2:* Pipe dots; sugar on wet piping.

2 **YELLOW OUTLINE FLOWER** Pipe outline and center dots; sugar on wet piped dots.

3 **BLUE AND YELLOW FLOWER** *Layer 1:* Pipe and flood; let dry. *Layer 2:* Pipe petal outlines and center; sugar on wet piping.

4 **BLUE FILIGREE FLOWER** Pipe filigree pattern; sugar on wet piping.

5 **SPARKLING DOTTED FLOWER** See cookie 1.

6 **SPARKLING BLUE FLOWER** *Layer 1:* Pipe and flood; let dry. *Layer 2:* Pipe petal outlines and center; sugar on wet piping.

7 **BLUE AND YELLOW OUTLINE FLOWER** Pipe petal outlines on plain cookie; affix dragees with piping icing.

8 **SPARKLING YELLOW FLOWER** Pipe center and leaf details; flood center; sugar entire cookie on wet flood and piping.

9 **PLAID FLOWER** Pipe first color line in crosshatch pattern; pipe second color over first; affix dragees to wet piping.

10 **BLUE FLOWER** *Layer 1:* Pipe and flood; let dry. *Layer 2:* Pipe outline; affix dragees to wet piping.

EASTER AND SPRING

Celebrate rebirth and nature's reawakening with a pastel icing palette and traditional symbols of Easter and spring. Egg shapes are perfect for creative interpretation and are great for filling Easter baskets — why not "dye" cookie eggs this year?

cookies featured

1 *Easter basket;* **2** *Pink Easter egg;* **3** *Yellow flower;* **4** *Watering can;* **5** *Pink flower;* **6** *Double-cookie yellow hat;* **7** *Easter bunny;* **8** *Polka-dot egg;* **9** *Small fancy Easter egg;* **10** *Chick*

decorating instructions

1 **EASTER BASKET** *Layer 1:* Pipe and flood top third of the cookie; sprinkle flower-shaped paillettes on wet flood; let dry. *Layer 2:* Using small basketweave tip, pipe basketweave pattern on bottom two-thirds of cookie. Pipe basket handle and border using the same tip and a ribbon motion.

2 **PINK EASTER EGG** Pipe and flood. Flood horizontal stripes on wet flood; draw toothpick from bottom to top of egg; repeat at intervals.

3 **YELLOW FLOWER** *Layer 1:* Pipe and flood; let dry. *Layer 2:* Pipe outline with contrasting color. Pipe dots in center.

4 **WATERING CAN** Pipe and flood watering-can shape, leaving space for "handle" and flowers. Sugar on wet flood. Affix flowers with piping icing.

5 **PINK FLOWER** *Layer 1:* Pipe and flood; let dry. *Layer 2:* Pipe outline with contrasting color. Pipe dots in center.

6 **DOUBLE-COOKIE YELLOW HAT** *Prebaking:* Stack smaller round on top of larger and bake. *After baking,* *layer 1:* Pipe and flood brim of hat; pipe and flood crown of hat; let dry. *Layer 2:* Using small leaf tip, pipe leaves around hat band; pipe dots in center of leaves. For a quicker cookie, skip the piping and flooding and simply create a colorful hat band!

7 **EASTER BUNNY** Pipe and flood; sprinkle jimmies on wet flood. Pipe rabbit ear, eye, and nose/whisker details.

8 **POLKA-DOT EGG** Pipe and flood. Flood dots on wet flood; sprinkle colorless sanding sugar on wet flood.

9 **SMALL FANCY EASTER EGG** *Layer 1:* Pipe and flood; let dry. *Layer 2:* Pipe lines, dots, and squiggles. For a quicker cookie and quicker cleanup, make chocolate cookie eggs, skip the flooding, and use zip-top bags to pipe lines, dots, and squiggles!

10 **CHICK** Pipe and flood; sprinkle orange sanding sugar on wet flood to create beak and feet. Pipe eye.

MOTHER'S DAY

Show Mom your appreciation for all she's done with a special cookie treat. If tea and bridge or fashionable hats aren't her thing, decorate cookie shapes that reflect her interests or hobbies. Of course, you could always make a three-dimensional cookie card that says how you feel.

cookies featured

1 *I ♥ MOM;* 2 *Periwinkle teapot;* 3 *Polka-dot hat;*
4 *Pearl necklace;* 5 *Teacup;* 6 *Purple teapot;*
7 *Dainty dotted hat;* 8 *Aqua teapot;* 9 *Pearl necklace*

decorating instructions

1 **I ♥ MOM** *Prebaking:* Cut out cookie letters and heart. Sugar unbaked cookie heart, then place on larger cookie; place letters on cookie. *After baking:* Paint letters with luster dust.

2 **PERIWINKLE TEAPOT** *Layer 1:* Pipe and flood; flood lid and base detail on wet flood; let dry. *Layer 2:* Pipe dots and lid detail.

3 **POLKA-DOT HAT** Use rolled fondant for hat and band (see chapter 6 for fondant technique).

4 **PEARL NECKLACE** Pipe and flood; affix pearl dragees to wet flood; let dry. Paint clasp with luster dust.

5 **TEACUP** *Layer 1:* Pipe and flood; flood stripes on wet flood; let dry. *Layer 2:* Pipe dots.

6 **PURPLE TEAPOT** *Prebaking:* Paint cookie with purple tempera paint. *After baking:* Paint lid and base details with luster dust.

7 **DAINTY DOTTED HAT** *Layer 1:* Pipe and flood; flood band on wet flood; let dry. *Layer 2:* Pipe dots.

8 **AQUA TEAPOT** *Layer 1:* Pipe and flood; flood lid and base detail on wet flood; let dry. *Layer 2:* Pipe loops and dot designs.

9 **PEARL NECKLACE** See cookie 4.

FATHER'S DAY

We've never met a dad who wasn't "wowed" by homemade cookies — especially if they were made just for him. For a golfer or sports fan, a businessman or do-it-himselfer, salute Father's Day by baking Dad a plateful of love.

cookies featured

1 *Hammer;* **2** *Football helmet;* **3** *Saw;* **4** *Football helmet;* **5** *Tie;* **6** *Sparkling football;* **7** *Football;* **8** *Putting green;* **9** *Hammer*

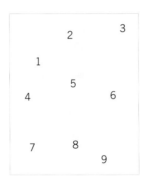

decorating instructions

1 HAMMER *Layer 1:* Pipe and flood handle in black; pipe and flood neck and head with white; let dry. *Layer 2:* Paint neck and head with silver luster dust. For a quicker cookie hammer, bake chocolate cookies, skip the royal icing, and paint the hammer neck and head with silver luster dust!

2 FOOTBALL HELMET *Layer 1:* Pipe and flood; let dry. *Layer 2:* Pipe helmet details.

3 SAW *Layer 1:* Pipe and flood handle in black; affix dragees. Pipe and flood blade in white; let dry. *Layer 2:* Paint blade with luster dust.

4 FOOTBALL HELMET See cookie 2.

5 TIE Pipe and flood collar; pipe and flood tie; flood stripes on wet flood. Add your own inscription, such as "#1 Dad!"

6 SPARKLING FOOTBALL Pipe and flood; sugar on wet flood; let dry. Pipe lace details.

7 FOOTBALL Pipe and flood; let dry. Pipe lace details. For a quicker cookie and quicker cleanup, use chocolate dough, skip the flooding, and use a zip-top bag to pipe laces.

8 PUTTING GREEN *Prebaking:* Color dough green and cut out hole with drinking straw. *After baking:* Pipe flag and dotted line to hole; affix pearl dragee "golf ball" near hole.

9 HAMMER See cookie 1.

HALLOWEEN

There's a nip in the air. The leaves are crackling underfoot. Ghosts and witches will soon be knocking at your front door. These are omens . . . prime baking season is about to begin! Treat your favorite tricksters with spooky cookies — or host a cookie craft party for home-based Halloween fun.

cookies featured

1 *Black cat;* 2 *Sparkly ghost;* 3 *Jack-o'-lantern;*
4 *Skull;* 5 *Silver-eyed bat;* 6 *Orange spiderweb;*
7 *Silver-eyed bat;* 8 *Tombstone with pumpkin;*
9 *Orange spiderweb;* 10 *Owl;* 11 *Orange-eyed bat;*
12 *Tombstone*

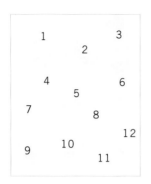

decorating instructions

1 **BLACK CAT** *Layer 1:* Pipe and flood. *Layer 2:* Pipe face and paw details on dry flood. For a simpler cookie, pipe the face and paws on a naked chocolate cookie.

2 **SPARKLY GHOST** Pipe and flood; flood dots on wet flood for face; sugar when flood is wet.

3 **JACK-O'-LANTERN** *Prebaking:* Color dough orange. *After baking:* Pipe and flood face. For more jack-o'-lantern inspirations, see the Thanksgiving pumpkins that follow.

4 **SKULL** Pipe and flood; flood eyes and nose on wet flood. Pipe mouth on wet flood.

5 **SILVER-EYED BAT** *Prebaking:* Imprint lines on wings; insert dragee eyes.

6 **ORANGE SPIDERWEB** Pipe and flood; flood circles on wet flood; draw toothpick through black circles.

7 **SILVER-EYED BAT** See cookie 5.

8 **TOMBSTONE WITH PUMPKIN** Pipe and flood each cookie separately. For tombstone: Use food-safe marker on dry flood. For pumpkin: Pipe details on dry flood. When both cookies are dry, attach pumpkin to tombstone with piping icing. *Tip:* When an easelback is affixed, tombstones make great place cards for Halloween parties. Write a clever "epitaph," such as "Here sits Scott." See chapter 7 for how-tos.

9 **ORANGE SPIDERWEB** See cookie 6.

10 **OWL** Pipe and flood; flood lines for wings on wet flood; draw toothpick through. Flood dark eye circles on wet flood; pipe irises and beak on wet flood.

11 **ORANGE-EYED BAT** Pipe wing detail; sugar on wet piping. Pipe eyes.

12 **TOMBSTONE** Pipe and flood. Use food-safe marker on dry flood. Write a clever "epitaph," such as "Here sits Scott."

cookie craft inspirations

THANKSGIVING AND AUTUMN

Family gatherings are the perfect time to showcase your cookie craft skills. Use pecans in your nutty rolled dough to give a fall texture and flavor to your Thanksgiving cookie plate. Cookies make great lunch-box treats with those leftover turkey sandwiches, too.

cookies featured

1 *Plain leaf;* **2** *Flooded leaf;* **3** *Black harvest-corn turkey;* **4** *Flooded leaf;* **5** *Plain leaf;* **6** *Flooded leaf;* **7** *Flooded leaf;* **8** *Leaf;* **9** *Black detailed pumpkin;* **10** *Large acorn;* **11** *Small acorn;* **12** *Plain leaf;* **13** *Candy-corn turkey;* **14** *Harvest pumpkin;* **15** *Front-facing pecan turkey;* **16** *Big black turkey;* **17** *Pumpkin;* **18** *Sparkly leaf;* **19** *Side-view pecan turkey;* **20** *Sparkly leaf;* **21** *Tie-dye leaf;* **22** *Small acorn;* **23** *Sparkly leaf;* **24** *Tie-dye leaf;* **25** *Pumpkin;* **26** *Sparkly leaf*

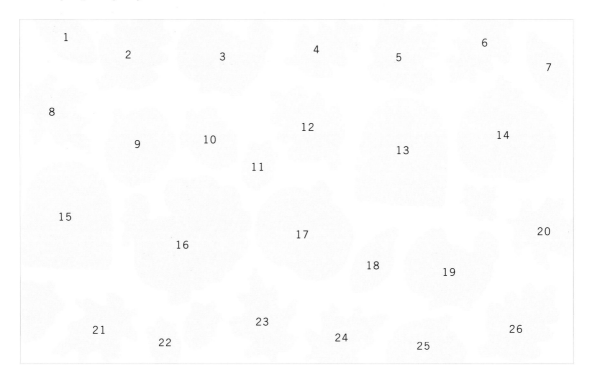

decorating instructions

1 **PLAIN LEAF** Pipe veins on plain cookie.

2 **FLOODED LEAF** *Layer 1:* Pipe and flood; let dry. *Layer 2:* Pipe veins.

3 **BLACK HARVEST-CORN TURKEY** *Layer 1:* Pipe and flood; flood stripes on wet flood in curved lines following turkey body contour. Draw toothpick perpendicular to lines from tail to neck to create feathers; affix first (outermost) layer of corn on wet flood; let dry. *Layer 2:* Pipe eye, wattle, and feet details; affix additional corn layers with piping icing.

4 **FLOODED LEAF** See cookie 2.

5 **PLAIN LEAF** See cookie 1.

6 **FLOODED LEAF** See cookie 2.

7 **FLOODED LEAF** See cookie 2.

8 **LEAF** Pipe and flood; flood veins on wet flood.

9 **BLACK DETAILED PUMPKIN** *Prebaking:* Color dough orange. *After baking:* Pipe contour details and stem. Sugar stem on wet piping.

10 **LARGE ACORN** *Prebaking:* Impress acorn cap details on nutty cookie by crisscrossing flat toothpick.

11 **SMALL ACORN** *Prebaking:* Sprinkle finely chopped nuts on acorn cap.

12 **PLAIN LEAF** See cookie 1.

13 **CANDY-CORN TURKEY** *Layer 1:* Pipe and flood turkey body shape; flood stripes on wet flood in a semicircle. Draw toothpick toward center, from bottom of body to neck, to create feathers; let dry. *Layer 2:* Affix candy corn to cookie with piping icing; pipe eye, beak, wattle, and feet.

14 **HARVEST PUMPKIN** *Layer 1:* Pipe and flood pumpkin and stem; let dry. *Layer 2:* Pipe contour lines; affix fondant leaf and vines with piping icing.

15 **FRONT-FACING PECAN TURKEY** *Prebaking:* Place rounds for turkey body; press nuts into dough for feathers. *After baking:* Pipe eyes, beak, wattle, and feet.

16 **BIG BLACK TURKEY** *Layer 1:* Pipe and flood; flood orange stripes in semicircles around tail area; flood gray stripes on body following contour. Draw toothpick through orange tail stripes from edge of cookie toward body; draw toothpick through gray stripes from neck toward tail. Flood two orange wing stripes; draw toothpick through wing stripes toward neck. Let dry. *Layer 2:* Pipe eye, wattle, and foot details.

17 **PUMPKIN** *Layer 1:* Pipe and flood pumpkin; let dry. *Layer 2:* Pipe and flood stem; sugar on wet flood; pipe pumpkin contours.

18 **SPARKLY LEAF** *Layer 1:* Pipe and flood; sugar on wet flood; let dry. *Layer 2:* Pipe veins.

19 **SIDE-VIEW PECAN TURKEY** *Prebaking:* Press pecan pieces into unbaked dough for feathers, eye, and wattle.

20 **SPARKLY LEAF** See cookie 18.

21 **TIE-DYE LEAF** Pipe and flood; flood veins on wet flood; draw toothpick through to create design.

22 **SMALL ACORN** See cookie 11.

23 **SPARKLY LEAF** See cookie 18.

24 **TIE-DYE LEAF** See cookie 21.

25 **PUMPKIN** *Layer 1:* Pipe and flood; let dry. *Layer 2:* Pipe contour lines; sugar on wet piping.

26 **SPARKLY LEAF** See cookie 18.

CHRISTMAS

'Tis the season for cookie crafting! Send a joyous cookie message, host a holiday cookie swap, or create a showstopping sleigh centerpiece. The simple gingerbread people, stars, and ornaments on page 31 are fun shapes for cookie crafters of all ages. Whether your cookies are laid out on a plate for Santa or packaged for giving, there's no time like the holidays for creating memorable homemade traditions.

cookies featured

1 *Gold ornament;* **2** *Green striped ornament;* **3** *Wreath;* **4** *Gold stocking;* **5** *Red polka-dot ornament;* **6** *Christmas tree with garland;* **7** *Wreath with sparkly berries;* **8** *Windowpane star;* **9** *Peace dove;* **10** *Candy cane;* **11** *Ornament;* **12** *Ornament;* **13** *Candy cane;* **14** *Red Dala horse;* **15** *Holly leaves;* **16** *Tree with dot ornaments;* **17** *Red stocking;* **18** *Gold Dala horse;* **19** *Green dotted ornament*

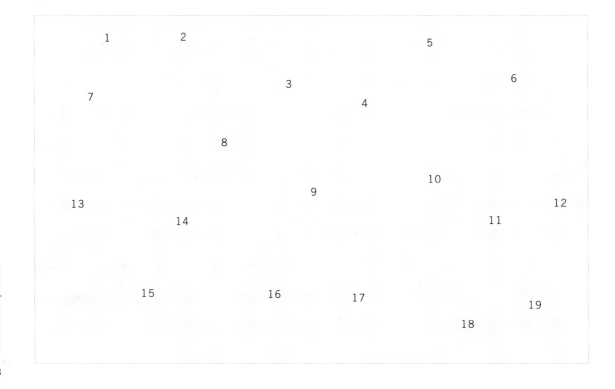

decorating instructions

1 **GOLD ORNAMENT** *Layer 1:* Pipe and flood; let dry. *Layer 2:* Paint entire cookie with luster dust; when dry, pipe dots; sugar on wet dots.

2 **GREEN STRIPED ORNAMENT** *Layer 1:* Pipe and flood; let dry. *Layer 2:* Pipe stripes; sugar on wet piping.

3 **WREATH** Pipe leaves using a leaf tip (such as a #67); pipe holly berry detail.

4 **GOLD STOCKING** *Layer 1:* Pipe and flood; let dry. *Layer 2:* Paint entire cookie with luster dust; when dry, pipe dots and cuff detail; sugar on wet piping.

5 **RED POLKA-DOT ORNAMENT** *Prebaking:* Poke hole in top of ornament. *After baking:* Pipe and flood; flood dots on wet flood. When dry, insert licorice whip.

6 **CHRISTMAS TREE WITH GARLAND** *Layer 1:* Pipe and flood; flood dots on wet flood; let dry. *Layer 2:* Pipe garland; sugar on wet piping.

7 **WREATH WITH SPARKLY BERRIES** *Layer 1:* Pipe leaves using a leaf tip (such as a #67); let dry. *Layer 2:* Pipe holly berry detail; sugar on wet piping.

8 **WINDOWPANE STAR** *Prebaking:* Cut hole in dough; fill with crushed hard candy (see chapter 5 for windowpane technique); bake and let cool. *After baking, layer 1:* Pipe and flood; let dry. *Layer 2:* Paint with luster dust.

9 **PEACE DOVE** *Layer 1:* Pipe and flood; let dry. *Layer 2:* Pipe olive branch detail.

10 **CANDY CANE** Pipe and flood; pipe lines on wet flood. Draw toothpick through lines.

11 **ORNAMENT** Pipe and flood; pipe lines on wet flood. Draw toothpick through lines. When dry, insert licorice whip.

12 **ORNAMENT** Pipe and flood; pipe lines on wet flood. Draw toothpick through lines.

13 **CANDY CANE** See cookie 10.

14 **RED DALA HORSE** *Layer 1:* Pipe and flood; flood mane dots on wet flood; draw toothpick through to make hearts. Drop dragees in wet flood to make saddle outline; let dry. *Layer 2:* Paint saddle detail with luster dust.

15 **HOLLY LEAVES** *Layer 1:* Pipe and flood; let dry. *Layer 2:* Pipe leaf detail; sugar on wet piping; pipe berries.

16 **TREE WITH DOT ORNAMENTS** *Layer 1:* Pipe and flood; drop dragees on wet flood; let dry. *Layer 2:* Pipe dot ornaments; pipe second color on dots.

17 **RED STOCKING** *Layer 1:* Pipe and flood white cuff; sprinkle jimmies. Pipe and flood red stocking body and loop; let dry. *Layer 2:* Pipe dots; sprinkle sugar on wet piping.

18 **GOLD DALA HORSE** *Layer 1:* Pipe and flood entire cookie. Flood dots on wet flood for saddle detail; draw toothpick through dots to make hearts; let dry. *Layer 2:* Paint luster dust on most of horse, leaving saddle. When dry, pipe dot detail around saddle and eye.

19 **GREEN DOTTED ORNAMENT** Pipe and flood; flood dots on wet flood; sugar on wet flood.

CHRISTMAS

cookies featured

1 *Christmas ornament;* **2** *Double sparkly star;* **3** *Christmas bulbs;* **4** *Sparkly star;* **5** *Mini Rudolphs;* **6** *Santa head;* **7** *Gingerbread man;* **8** *Holly wreath;* **9** *Sideways Santa;* **10** *Joy greeting;* **11** *Double sparkly star;* **12** *Gingerbread lady;* **13** *Christmas tree on truck;* **14** *Holly wreath*

decorating instructions

1. **CHRISTMAS ORNAMENT** *Prebaking:* Make sugar and gingerbread dough. Use drinking straw to cut out holes; use end of chopstick or skewer to impress dots. Use an aspic cutter to cut out small stars; place on unbaked gingerbread. Paint stars with tempera paint. Bake.

2. **DOUBLE SPARKLY STAR** *Prebaking:* Make sugar and gingerbread dough. Cut larger star in gingerbread; smaller star in sugar dough. Sprinkle smaller star with colored sugar and place on gingerbread star before baking.

3. **CHRISTMAS BULBS** *Prebaking:* Use drinking straw to cut out holes; drag flat toothpick to impress "screwtop" lines. *After baking:* Pipe and flood bulbs; paint screwtop with luster dust; let dry. String bulbs together with fresh and pliable licorice whip. If desired, to keep light bulbs in place on "string," knot licorice whip over each bulb.

4. **SPARKLY STAR** *Prebaking:* Sprinkle with colored sugar.

5. **MINI RUDOLPHS** Pipe red noses on baked cookies.

6. **SANTA HEAD** *Layer 1:* Pipe and flood red hat; pipe and flood white hat trim, and beard; let dry. *Layer 2:* Pipe nose, cheeks, eyes, and hat pom-pom.

7. **GINGERBREAD MAN** *Prebaking:* Press dried fruit into dough (if fruit is too big, use scissors to cut). Using heart-shaped aspic cutter as guide, sprinkle colored sugar into heart shape.

8. **HOLLY WREATH** Pipe and flood. Flood green lines on wet flood. Draw toothpick through lines to create leaf points. Flood red dots on wet flood.

9. **SIDEWAYS SANTA** *Layer 1:* Pipe and flood red suit and hat and white sack and beard, leaving face un-iced. Pipe and flood black boots. *Layer 2:* Pipe pom-pom, cuffs, and "curl" detail on beard. Pipe gift; pipe gloves, belt, and eyes. Pipe nose, ribbon on gift, and outline on suit and hat.

10. **JOY GREETING** *Pre-baking:* Cut out J, O, and Y with mini letter cutters. *After baking:* Pipe details around letters and on background.

11. **DOUBLE SPARKLY STAR** See cookie 2.

12. **GINGERBREAD LADY** *Layer 1:* Pipe and flood pinafore; let dry. *Layer 2:* Pipe hearts, hair, eyes, and mouth.

13. **CHRISTMAS TREE ON TRUCK** *Layer 1:* Pipe and flood red truck body, and white window and headlight. Pipe and flood black tires, leaving hubcap un-iced. *Layer 2:* Pipe truck outline. Pipe Christmas tree. Paint hubcaps with luster dust.

14. **HOLLY WREATH** See cookie 8.

HANUKKAH

Cookies are always welcome at Hanukkah gatherings of family and friends and as gifts for one or more of the eight nights of the festival. Traditional Jewish symbols such as the Star of David and the Torah can also be used for bar mitzvah or bat mitzvah favors.

cookies featured

1 *Blue Star of David;* **2** *Sparkling dreidel;*
3 *Sparkling menorah;* **4** *Dreidel;* **5** *White and silver Torah;* **6** *Sparkling menorah;* **7** *Silver dreidel;*
8 *Sparkling menorah;* **9** *Dreidel;* **10** *White sparkling Star of David;* **11** *Dreidel;* **12** *Blue Star of David;*
13 *White sparkling Torah;* **14** *Blue sparkling Star of David*

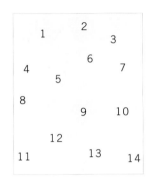

decorating instructions

1 **BLUE STAR OF DAVID** *Layer 1:* Pipe and flood; let dry. *Layer 2:* Pipe detail.

2 **SPARKLING DREIDEL** *Layer 1:* Pipe and flood; sugar on wet flood; let dry. *Layer 2:* Pipe detail.

3 **SPARKLING MENORAH** *Layer 1:* Pipe and flood entire menorah; let dry. *Layer 2:* Pipe and flood menorah base; pipe candles; sugar on wet icing. Affix dragees to wet icing as candle flames.

4 **DREIDEL** *Layer 1:* Pipe and flood; let dry. *Layer 2:* Pipe details.

5 **WHITE AND SILVER TORAH** *Layer 1:* Pipe and flood; let dry. *Layer 2:* Pipe detail; paint ends with luster dust.

6 **SPARKLING MENORAH** See cookie 3.

7 **SILVER DREIDEL** *Layer 1:* Pipe and flood; let dry. *Layer 2:* Paint with luster dust; pipe details.

8 **SPARKLING MENORAH** See cookie 3.

9 **DREIDEL** See cookie 4.

10 **WHITE SPARKLING STAR OF DAVID** *Layer 1:* Pipe and flood; let dry. *Layer 2:* Pipe outline detail; sugar on wet piping.

11 **DREIDEL** See cookie 4.

12 **BLUE STAR OF DAVID** See cookie 1.

13 **WHITE SPARKLING TORAH** *Layer 1:* Pipe and flood scroll body; let dry. *Layer 2:* Pipe detail; sugar on wet piping.

14 **BLUE SPARKLING STAR OF DAVID** *Layer 1:* Pipe and flood; sugar on wet flood; let dry. *Layer 2:* Pipe outline detail. For a quicker cookie, sugar the cookie before baking; when cool, pipe detail using a zip-top bag.

cookie craft for celebrations

Commemorate life's celebrations with cookies designed with the occasion in mind. Weddings, babies, milestone birthdays — even a bon voyage for that special trip — provide opportunities to create thoughtful, beautiful, or whimsical cookie favors or gifts. For celebrations focused around the table, why not make stand-up cookie place cards — you'll find the how-to instructions in chapter 7.

SHOWERS AND WEDDINGS

The events surrounding nuptial rituals are perfect for cookie-crafted favors. From wedding rings to a replica of a wedding cake, cookies add joy to an already sweet celebration. Choose classically beautiful white-on-white decorations, or match the bridesmaids' dress color.

cookies featured

1 *Wedding rings;* **2** *Jimmy-bodice wedding gown;* **3** *Umbrella;* **4** *Heart-topped wedding cake;* **5** *Umbrella;* **6** *Pink gift box;* **7** *Dotted wedding gown;* **8** *Heart cutout bridesmaid's dress;* **9** *Wedding cake*

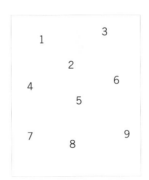

decorating instructions

1 **WEDDING RINGS** *Prebaking:* Cut out rounds within rounds. Overlap rings on cookie sheet; bake and let cool. *After baking:* Paint with luster dust.

2 **JIMMY-BODICE WEDDING GOWN** *Layer 1:* Pipe and flood; sprinkle bodice with jimmies; let dry. *Layer 2:* Pipe detail; sugar on wet piping.

3 **UMBRELLA** *Layer 1:* Pipe and flood; let dry. *Layer 2:* Pipe detail; sugar on wet piping.

4 **HEART-TOPPED WEDDING CAKE** *Layer 1:* Pipe and flood heart; sugar on wet flood. Pipe and flood remainder of cake shape; let dry. *Layer 2:* Pipe detail; sugar on wet piping.

5 **UMBRELLA** See cookie 3.

6 **PINK GIFT BOX** *Layer 1:* Pipe and flood box; let dry. *Layer 2:* Pipe box outline detail; with flat pastry tip, pipe ribbon.

7 **DOTTED WEDDING DRESS** *Layer 1:* Pipe and flood; sugar on wet flood; let dry. *Layer 2:* Pipe dot details.

8 **HEART CUTOUT BRIDESMAID'S DRESS** *Prebaking:* Cut out hearts at hem of dress; bake. *After baking: layer 1:* Pipe and flood; let dry. *Layer 2:* Pipe details; sugar on wet piping. *Hint:* Use heart cutouts to adorn other cookie shapes!

9 **WEDDING CAKE** *Layer 1:* Pipe and flood; let dry. *Layer 2:* Paint with pearl dust; pipe detail; affix dragees to wet piping.

Honor the birthday guy or gal with specially crafted cookies. Say "hi" to your new neighbor with an edible welcome. A champagne-bottle cookie cutter is handy for congratulatory occasions of all kinds, and a set of number cutters will help celebrate a lifetime of birthdays and anniversaries.

cookies featured

1 *Silver jeweled crown;* **2** *Bon voyage plane;* **3** *Gold crown;* **4** *New home;* **5** *Sweet 16;* **6** *Champagne bottle;* **7** *Gold cutout crown;* **8** *Bon voyage suitcase*

decorating instructions

1 **SILVER JEWELED CROWN** *Prebaking:* Cut out jewel shapes; place on raw cookie crown. Bake and let cool. *After baking:* Paint with luster dust. Affix dragee with piping icing.

2 **BON VOYAGE PLANE** *Layer 1:* Pipe and flood; let dry. *Layer 2:* Paint plane with luster dust; pipe details.

3 **GOLD CROWN** Paint with luster dust. Affix dragees with piping icing.

4 **NEW HOME** *Prebaking:* Impress door, window, and siding. *After baking:* Paint roof, chimney, and door with luster dust. For a new neighbor, you can also add "Welcome" or "New Home" in piped letters.

5 **SWEET 16** Pipe and flood; flood dots on wet flood. Any special birthday or anniversary can be commemorated with number cookies.

6 **CHAMPAGNE BOTTLE** *Layer 1:* Paint neck and cap of bottle with luster dust; pipe and flood label in white; pipe "vintage" year (year of honoree's birth or marriage) on wet flood; let dry. *Layer 2:* Pipe and flood label in gold, around "vintage" year and slightly inside of white label (to leave edges). For another style of champagne bottle, see New Year's cookies on page 7.

7 **GOLD CUTOUT CROWN** *Prebaking:* Cut out jewel shapes; bake and let cool. *After baking:* Paint with luster dust; affix dragee with piping icing. *Hint:* Use cutouts for silver jeweled crown!

8 **BON VOYAGE SUITCASE** *Layer 1:* Pipe and flood; let dry. *Layer 2:* Pipe handle.

NEW BABY OR BABY SHOWER

Fete the impending or newly arrived bundle of joy with an assortment of crafted cookies. Teddy bears and rocking horses bring smiles; baby carriages can be made into boxes for favors (page 119). In a pastel palette, umbrellas (see also pages 36–37) are baby shower appropriate.

cookies featured

1 *Bottle;* **2** *Onesie;* **3** *Umbrella;* **4** *Teddy bear;* **5** *Bib;* **6** *Pink carriage;* **7** *Blue carriage;* **8** *Rocking horse;* **9** *Bottle*

decorating instructions

1 **BOTTLE** *Layer 1:* Pipe and flood; let dry. *Layer 2:* Pipe detail.

2 **ONESIE** *Layer 1:* Pipe and flood; let dry. *Layer 2:* Pipe detail.

3 **UMBRELLA** *Layer 1:* Pipe and flood; sugar handle on wet flood; let dry. *Layer 2:* Pipe detail.

4 **TEDDY BEAR** Pipe and flood bib; sugar on wet flood.

5 **BIB** *Layer 1:* Pipe and flood bib shape on round cookie; pipe tie; let dry. *Layer 2:* Pipe dots.

6 **PINK CARRIAGE** *Layer 1:* Pipe and flood; let dry. *Layer 2:* Pipe carriage outline and wheels; sugar on wet piping; pipe dots.

7 **BLUE CARRIAGE** *Layer 1:* Pipe and flood; let dry. *Layer 2:* Pipe dots; sugar on wet piping; pipe outline and wheels.

8 **ROCKING HORSE** *Layer 1:* Pipe and flood entire cookie; let dry. *Layer 2:* Pipe and flood horse and rocker; sugar on wet flood; let dry. *Layer 3:* Pipe mane and tail; sugar on wet piping. Pipe eye, reins, and dots. For a quicker cookie, skip the first layer of piping and flooding; you will see the cookie through the rocker.

9 **BOTTLE** See cookie 1.

Kids and cookies are a natural combination — celebrate their special day with cookies crafted just for them, or host a decorating party and have their friends join the decorating fun (see chapter 9).

cookies featured

1 *Basketball;* **2** *Dinosaur;* **3** *Baseball;* **4** *Baseball;* **5** *Astronaut;* **6** *Alphabet block;* **7** *Dinosaur;* **8** *Tennis ball;* **9** *Rocket ship;* **10** *Astronaut;* **11** *Basketball;* **12** *Baseball*

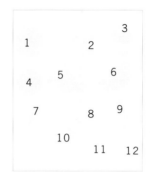

decorating instructions

1 **BASKETBALL** *Layer 1:* Pipe and flood; let dry. *Layer 2:* Pipe detail.

2 **DINOSAUR** Pipe and flood; flood dots on wet flood.

3 **BASEBALL** *Layer 1:* Pipe and flood; let dry. *Layer 2:* Pipe detail.

4 **BASEBALL** See cookie 3.

5 **ASTRONAUT** *Prebaking:* Use gingerbread-man cookie cutter. *After baking, layer 1:* Pipe and flood, leaving faceplate open; let dry. *Layer 2:* Pipe spacesuit details; paint gloves, boots, and faceplate with luster dust. Use piping icing to affix licorice whip for lifeline; affix lifeline to rocket ship.

6 **ALPHABET BLOCK** *Layer 1:* Pipe and flood; let dry. *Layer 2:* Pipe letters; sugar on wet piping; pipe block edges.

7 **DINOSAUR** See cookie 2.

8 **TENNIS BALL** *Layer 1:* Pipe and flood; let dry. *Layer 2:* Pipe detail.

9 **ROCKET SHIP** *Layer 1:* Pipe and flood; place dragees on wet flood; let dry. *Layer 2:* Paint stripe between dragees with luster.

10 **ASTRONAUT** See cookie 5.

11 **BASKETBALL** See cookie 1.

12 **BASEBALL** See cookie 3.

GIRLFRIENDS

Girls just want to have fun! Next time the ladies lunch, have their favorite accessories at the ready to munch on (a cocktail is one of *our* favorites, anyway . . .). Channel your inner Coco Chanel and go wild decorating your cookie dresses.

cookies featured

1 *Small purse;* **2** *Flowered dress;* **3** *Large purse;*
4 *Small purse;* **5** *Shopping bag;* **6** *Frosty cosmopolitan;* **7** *Shirley Temple;* **8** *Sparkling purse;*
9 *Collared dress*

decorating instructions

1 **SMALL PURSE** *Prebaking:* Use small flat-bottomed oval cutter. *After baking, layer 1:* Pipe and flood purse rectangle; let dry. *Layer 2:* Pipe purse outline and flap; pipe dots for handle and detail, if desired; affix dragee with piping icing for clasp.

2 **FLOWERED DRESS** *Layer 1:* Pipe and flood; flood flower center dots on wet flood; let dry. *Layer 2:* Pipe dots around neckline, arms, and hem. Pipe dot details around flower centers and between flowers.

3 **LARGE PURSE** *Layer 1:* Pipe and flood purse body and handle; let dry. *Layer 2:* Pipe outline detail; affix dragee with piping icing for clasp.

4 **SMALL PURSE** See cookie 1.

5 **SHOPPING BAG** *Prebaking:* Cut out holes for licorice handle using drinking straw. *After baking, layer 1:* Pipe and flood; let dry. *Layer 2:* Lace licorice whip through holes; tie knot in back of cookie; pipe logo.

6 **FROSTY COSMOPOLITAN** Pipe and flood "drink" portion; carefully paint corn syrup on remainder of cookie; sprinkle entire cookie with sanding sugar; let dry.

7 **SHIRLEY TEMPLE** Pipe and flood; flood cherry on wet flood.

8 **SPARKLING PURSE** *Layer 1:* Pipe and flood purse body and handle; sugar on wet flood; let dry. *Layer 2:* Pipe outline detail; affix dragee with piping icing for clasp.

9 **COLLARED DRESS** *Layer 1:* Pipe and flood; let dry. *Layer 2:* Pipe detail.

PETS

Welcome a furry new addition to the family, or thank your pet sitter or veterinarian with a tin of man's best friends or fabulous felines. For that special pet owner — or someone who's on your "list"! — personalize the doghouse with a food-safe marker or piped icing. If you're an experienced cookie crafter, you can even create an animal "portrait" with the color and pattern of the pet's coat.

cookies featured

1 *Paw print;* **2** *Sparkling spotted dog;* **3** *Sparkling dog bone;* **4** *Elegant cat;* **5** *Paw print;* **6** *Doghouse;* **7** *Fire hydrant;* **8** *Sparkling cat;* **9** *Dalmatian;* **10** *Dog bone;* **11** *Fire hydrant*

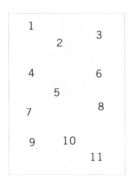

decorating instructions

1 **PAW PRINT** *Layer 1:* Pipe and flood; let dry. *Layer 2:* Pipe and flood "pads"; sugar on wet flood. For a quicker cookie, omit layer 1; pipe and flood pads on plain cookie.

2 **SPARKLING SPOTTED DOG** *Layer 1:* Pipe and flood; let dry. *Layer 2:* Pipe and flood spots, eye, and nose; sugar on wet flood.

3 **SPARKLING DOG BONE** Pipe and flood; sugar on wet flood.

4 **ELEGANT CAT** *Prebaking:* Imprint face; press in pearl dragees for collar.

5 **PAW PRINT** See cookie 1.

6 **DOGHOUSE** *Layer 1:* Pipe and flood; let dry. *Layer 2:* Pipe and flood roof and door; sugar on wet flood. Pipe siding and dog name.

7 **FIRE HYDRANT** *Layer 1:* Pipe and flood; let dry. *Layer 2:* Pipe detail.

8 **SPARKLING CAT** *Layer 1:* Pipe and flood; flood stripes and eyes on wet flood; sugar on wet flood; let dry. *Layer 2:* Pipe eyes and mouth.

9 **DALMATIAN** Pipe and flood; flood dots on wet flood; pipe nose and mouth.

10 **DOG BONE** Pipe and flood.

11 **FIRE HYDRANT** See cookie 7.

2

ingredients, supplies, and equipment

The beauty of cookie baking is that you probably already have most of the ingredients and much of the equipment you'll need — but it's like the old story of stone soup: A man can make soup with just his magic stone, but it would be *a little bit better* with some carrot. . . . Then, though it tastes great, gee, *if you only had some barley.* . . . Once you get started with cookie crafting, you'll find you want additional tools and supplies to make the process a bit easier. Following are lists of the ingredients, supplies, and equipment that are both necessary and very helpful.

COOKIE INGREDIENTS

* **FLOUR.** We've tested a variety of flours, and we have our own preferences. Your favorite brand of all-purpose will do just fine.

* **GRANULATED SUGAR.** Again, use whatever you usually use for baking.

* **BUTTER.** Of course, we like to avoid trans fats/hydrogenated oils, but the real reason to use butter is that nothing beats the taste of a real butter cookie. Janice usually buys organic; Valerie buys what's on sale. Either way, use unsalted so that you can control the amount of salt in the recipe. It's not a tragedy, however, if all you have in the fridge is salted.

* **EGGS.** Size matters a bit; try to use large eggs for all recipes.

* **FRESH CITRUS.** Lemon, lime, or orange zest really brightens the flavor of sugar cookies, and fresh lemon juice is our preferred royal icing flavor (though you can try lime or orange juice or use an extract).

* **EXTRACTS.** Vanilla extract is almost universally appealing. According to your own tastes, you can also use almond extract, peppermint extract (good for candy-cane cookies), or any others you find.

* **COCOA POWDER.** Because we don't use leavening in our chocolate cookie recipe, you can make it with either natural (nonalkalized) cocoa powder or alkalized (Dutch-process or Dutched) cocoa. Natural cocoa powder includes brands such as Hershey's, Nestle, and Ghirardelli — that is, any brand containing 100 percent cocoa. Alkalized (Dutch-process cocoa) — such as Droste or Hershey's Dutch-Process — may react differently with leavening. It's especially delicious used in our recipe, but be aware that in many recipes it is not interchangeable with natural cocoa.

* **ESPRESSO POWDER.** This is the fancy term for instant espresso coffee. It deepens the overall flavor of chocolate cookies and makes them taste more chocolaty (never a bad thing). We use the Medaglia D'Oro that we find in our neighborhood supermarket, but feel free to use whatever brand your local supermarket carries or use instant coffee as a substitute.

ICING INGREDIENTS

* **CONFECTIONERS' (POWDERED) SUGAR.** The 1-pound box is the amount the larger royal icing recipe calls for, so no measuring!

* **EGG-WHITE PRODUCTS.** Any of the three mentioned below will work, so just use the one most convenient for you. Our royal icing recipes (chapter 6) call for one of them instead of raw egg whites because they streamline the icing-making process and eliminate worry about salmonella.

  Powdered egg whites. If you've never made royal icing before, this is one ingredient you probably don't have in your pantry. A tub of powdered egg whites makes many recipes and has a long shelf life. Deb-El's product called Just Whites is available in some supermarkets; the powdered egg white from CK Products can be found in specialty cooking stores. Dollar for dollar, powdered egg whites are the best value and have the longest shelf life of any egg-white product.

  Liquid pasteurized egg whites. Brands such as All Whites from Papetti Foods are widely available in your supermarket's dairy case, near the eggs and egg substitutes. These are easy to work with, and because they're pasteurized, they present no danger of salmonella.

  Meringue powder. This is made of powdered egg whites and sugar and/or stabilizers. Right now, few supermarkets carry it, but it's widely available online or in the specialty cooking stores noted in the resources (page 154).

* **LIGHT CORN SYRUP.** This is good for making fondant adhere to the cookie and to ensure that decorative sugars stick to the cookie after baking.

* **COLORINGS.** Be forewarned that all the colorings discussed here can stain. Use caution when mixing, and wear an apron. No matter how careful we think we are when we mix, we always wind up wearing a blob of color somewhere. Also note that the colors will stain wooden utensils; it's best to use metal for mixing and stirring.

  Liquid food coloring. Available in your supermarket, this is the stuff you grew up with: Weenie in Yonkers always used McCormick and Mildred in Los Angeles always had Schilling. The two were always the same company, but now they just go by the name McCormick. The classic box still contains red, green, blue, and yellow, with instructions on how to mix other colors. This liquid food coloring is handy and versatile and can even be used for coloring your own sugars and coconut (see page 53).

The nice customer-service lady at McCormick was happy to let us share the company's color-blending chart in case you've lost the box your food coloring came in. If you want stronger colors than you achieve with the number of drops indicated, multiply the drops proportionately. For example, for a deeper orange, use 4 drops of yellow (instead or 2) and 2 drops of red (instead of 1).

COLOR-BLENDING CHART	MIX (IN DROPS)			
	GREEN	YELLOW	RED	BLUE
ORANGE		2	1	
PURPLE			3	1
TURQUOISE	1			3
CHARTREUSE	1	12		
TOAST	1	4	3	
VIOLET			1	2

FOR THIS COLOR

Gels. These are widely available at cooking specialty shops, at craft shops, and online, under brands such as Ateco and Wilton. We like the ones that come in handy squeeze bottles because they give deep, saturated color and are the easiest colorings to use. As in a box of Crayolas, there is a wide assortment of colors available. Often, there are dots of color on the tops of the bottles to indicate what's inside, but we've found these are merely a guide; be aware that they don't exactly represent the color you wind up with after you mix the gel with the icing or dough. Before using a gel, then, make sure you read the name of the color on the label — we've found that something with a pink dot might be closer to purple when the gel is mixed, and the name will indicate this.

ADDITIONAL PANTRY SUPPLIES TO HAVE ON HAND

❋ **LUSTER DUST AND PEARL DUST.** These powders must be mixed with a clear spirit (such as vodka) to create shiny or pearly "paint." The spirit evaporates and leaves behind a saturated, opaque metallic sheen. The powders come in a variety of colors.

❋ **SUGARS AND SUGARLIKE ADD-ONS.** There are a zillion (count 'em!) different shapes and colors you can add on to your cookies — either before or after baking — to complete their look, and there will probably be a few more invented by the time you read this. While we describe here the general types of decorations available, a trip to your favorite baking supply store or Web site will inspire your own inventions.

Ready-to-use *colored sugar* is available in pretty much any color and in a variety of crystal sizes.

ingredients, supplies, and equipment

COLORING YOUR OWN
SUGAR AND COCONUT

If you've already invested in food colorings, it's incredibly easy and inexpensive to make your own colored sugar and coconut. You can use white household sugar or, for more sparkle, white sanding sugar (see the resources on page 154 for bulk suppliers). Simply place the desired amount of sugar or flaked coconut in a sandwich-sized zip-top bag. We suggest starting with 2 to 3 tablespoons; you can always make more. Add a drop or two of the food coloring, then seal the bag and massage it to mix the ingredients. In a couple of minutes, the coloring will evenly saturate the sugar or coconut.

If you're using gel coloring (which is more vibrant than liquid food coloring), a drop may be all you need. If you're using liquid food coloring, you may need a bit more. (Refer to the color chart on page 52 for the proportions needed to make various colors.) Remember, it's easy to add more color but impossible to take it out, so start with less and add as needed.

Sugar with larger crystals, called *sanding sugar,* sparkles more. While you can buy colored sugar, it's very simple and easier on your wallet to make your own. (See page 53.) *Sprinkles* or *nonpareils* are the tiny spheres we all know and love. *Jimmies,* tiny rod-shaped candies, are the standard sundae-toppers. They come in many color combinations and are sometimes mixed with confetti. The flat sugar shapes known as *confetti* or *paillettes* now come in a huge variety of shapes, from bunnies to pumpkins and everything in between. The spheres called *dragees* are most often coated with silver but also come in white, pastels, copper, and gold. **NOTE:** The FDA considers the metallic colors to be safe only for decoration.

* **OTHER ADD-ONS.** These include nuts, candies, coconut, fruit leather, and mini chips — we've even used pretzels. If you plan on adding any of these before baking cookies, keep in mind that heat might alter the characteristics of add-ons that aren't specifically designed for baking. (See Test First! on page 92.)

* **FONDANT.** This sugar-based decorating medium has recently come back into fashion. Though making your own is tricky and cumbersome, ready-made fondant is now widely available in a variety of colors at baking supply stores and many craft stores. With fondant, it's easy to achieve beautiful, vibrant cookies. (See chapter 6, page 111, for information on working with fondant.) Be forewarned, however:

The substance has a bland, sugary taste and chewy texture, and we don't love to eat it. Therefore, rather than using it to completely cover our cookies, we prefer to use it for details.

EQUIPMENT

As you'll see here, you can make attractively decorated cookies with not much more than a plastic bag and a recipe of royal icing. With less than a 20-dollar investment for supplies, however, you can make your cookie decorating both efficient and easy. Many of these items are available at your local kitchen shop or craft store, but in case you can't find something, the resources on page 154 include Internet and catalog sources for everything mentioned here.

* **ELECTRIC MIXER.** We love our heavy-duty stand mixers, but we know that people made cookies for hundreds of years before mixers were invented. If you don't have one, just be prepared to use a lot of elbow grease to mix the dough. You will need at least an electric hand mixer for the royal icing.

* **MIXING BOWLS.** Of course, if you're using a stand mixer, the work bowl comes with it. We bought ourselves extra stand mixer bowls, so that when we're making multiple batches or we're mixing royal icing, we don't have to stop and wash up. If you're not using a stand mixer, make sure your bowl is large enough to hold all ingredients with room to spare so you can mix without getting the contents all over your countertop.

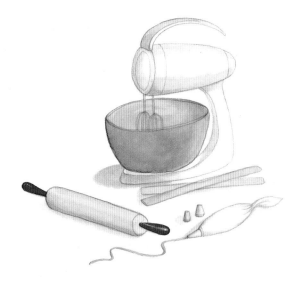

* **COOKIE SLATS.** This is our name for the strips of wood that we use to ensure that our dough or fondant is a uniform thickness as we roll it. While not mandatory, cookie slats have changed our cookie-baking lives and we highly recommend using them. You can get wood strips, sometimes called lattice slats or lumber scants, in hardware or craft stores. For cookies, slats should be ¼ inch thick, 2 feet long, and 2 inches wide; for fondant, slats should be ⅛ inch thick. Buy two of each size (they're inexpensive) and give them a light rinse and wipe before you use them the first time and after each use. (Be careful not to soak them; they might warp.) There are also several commercial products available to help keep your cookies an even thickness (though they are more expensive than slats). For example, Perfection Strips are the plastic version of cookie slats. The Dobord is a big board with adjustable edges that allows you to roll dough to a precise thickness. Rolling-pin rings are designed to go on the ends of your rolling pin to control dough thickness — but be forewarned that we found these tricky to use depending on the diameter of the rolling pin.

* **MEASURING CUPS AND SPOONS.** If you're new to baking, make sure you use dry measuring cups for flour and sugars. These come in sets containing measures for ¼ cup, ⅓ cup, ½ cup, and 1 cup. Here's how to measure dry ingredients (for example, flour or sugar): Scoop the ingredient into your measuring cup, then level it off with the straight edge of a knife. Don't pack it unless the recipe instructs you to do so (as it may for brown sugar). Cups used to measure liquids are most often clear glass or plastic with volume markings for ounces or fluid-cup increments. Use these for measuring molasses, corn syrup, or other liquids.

* **WAX PAPER.** We use this to roll out the cookies, which eliminates the need for flouring the rolling surface, cutting down on mess and minimizing the drying out of cookie dough. It's also useful for packing cookies for freezing or shipping (see chapter 8).

* **ROLLING PIN.** Whatever kind you choose (wooden, marble, silicone), it should be straight and not tapered (that is, the circumference must be consistent along the length of the pin) to ensure that the dough is a consistent thickness as you roll. We've had our rolling pins forever, but when researching rolling pins, we noticed that you can spend nearly

GIFT IDEA
FOR A NEW COOKIE CRAFTER

For your fellow creative types who haven't yet expressed themselves in the cookie medium, a cookie-decorating kit makes a great gift. Include the following:

* ✻ 4 #2 decorating tips
* ✻ 4 couplers
* ✻ 1 package of disposable pastry bags
* ✻ 4 squeeze bottles
* ✻ 2 cookie slats (¼ inch thick by 24 inches long)
* ✻ food coloring gels
* ✻ cookie cutters
* ✻ powdered egg white
* ✻ 1 copy of *Cookie Craft* (of course)

60 dollars on a professional-quality model, although you can also find them for less than 10 dollars. Many rolling pins have a larger circumference, but 2 inches is the French rolling-pin standard.

✳ **COOKIE CUTTERS.** The more the merrier! Cookie cutters come in hundreds of shapes and are widely available starting at about a dollar apiece for tin. (Some specialty Web sites have cutters starting as low as 49 cents!) We like having a selection of versatile shapes on hand for our improvisation — for example, circle cutters in all sizes are quite useful (see page 140) for some of the cookie possibilities with round cutters; and note that biscuit cutters and even a glass, in a pinch, can work for circles, too). Squares and rectangles are useful, too. We also love mini aspic cutters made by Ateco, which can be used to create decorative cutouts and dimensional add-ons (see chapter 4, pages 90–91). These can also be used for sugaring (see chapter 4, page 93). There are even cutters that you can use to create three-dimensional, stand-up cookies such as reindeer and trees. Check the resources section for Web sites and places that sell a selection of cutters, and see Keeping Track of Your Cookie Cutters on page 58 for hints on how to create a handy reference for your cookie-cutter inventory. Though cutters are by far the easiest way to create cookie shapes, we've

included templates (pages 152–153) for the flat-bottomed oval we use for cookie heads, turkeys, and tombstones and the shapes we use for easelbacks for stand-up cookies (see page 117).

✳ **COOKIE SHEETS.** We have every type of cookie sheet known to bakers — double-layer, ridged, sheets with silicone feet — but we almost always use what's known as a half-sheet or jelly roll pan. Its bottom surface is 11½ inches wide by 16½ inches long and it has a lip all the way around the edge, which makes it easier to remove it from the oven and prevents the cookies from sliding off the pan. Of course, any cookie sheet you have is just fine to use, but if you have darker, nonstick sheets, be careful: The bottoms of the cookies tend to brown very quickly on

If you're like us, all your cookie cutters are in a big plastic box, and you tend to forget what you already have — but you can easily create a chart to keep track of your shapes and sizes. Store it in your cookie box for immediate reference as you plan. If you're computer savvy, you can use a spreadsheet program (such as Excel). The chart can be sorted by occasion or shape, whichever works best for you. If you think this level of organization is a bit much, just wait: Your list will inspire ideas and will save you from buying the same cookie cutter twice — and you won't have to dig through your jumbled box of cutters just to remember what's there. If you have a lot of cutters, it's also helpful to store them within the box in large zip-top bags, labeled by the main occasion. This will come in handy when you're baking for winter and are able to grab one bag with all your winter cutters.

Your chart might look something like this:

MY COOKIE CUTTERS			
SHAPE	SIZE AND NOTES	PRIMARY OCCASION	OTHER OCCASIONS
TEDDY BEAR	2 INCHES, SMALL	CHRISTMAS	BABY SHOWER
CHAMPAGNE GLASS	4 INCHES, TALL	NEW YEAR'S	CONGRATULATIONS
SNOWFLAKE	3 INCHES	WINTER	CHRISTMAS

these. We recommend you use disposable alumi-num pans only in dire emergencies; they're too thin for the cookies to cook evenly, which means you'll have to watch your cookies like a hawk to make sure they don't burn.

✳ **PARCHMENT.** Not to be confused with wax paper (which will melt in the oven), baking parchment creates a nonstick surface for baking. If you've never used it, it will change your cookie life. It comes in rolls and is available in the supermarket in the food wrap section. Available online (and we love them) are precut sheets of parchment that handily fit half-sheet pans. If you use parchment, you can carefully slide the whole paper full of hot cookies from the pan onto a cooling rack, then cool the pan with cold water and dry it thoroughly so that it's ready to go in the oven again with a fresh batch of cookies. You can also work ahead and place a batch of unbaked cookies on a piece of parchment on the countertop, then just slide the parchment onto the next available cookie sheet. *Note:* We make sure to reuse our parchment paper. The folks at Reynolds recommend using parchment once on each side and only on the same day. (In other words, don't save a once-used piece for another baking day.)

✳ **SILICONE BAKING MATS.** With brand names such as Silpat and SiliconeZone, silicone baking mats are highly valued for their nonstick qualities and can be used for many baking purposes. In cookie baking, they're used the same way as parchment, but they do need to be cool before you place cookie dough on them. This means that in order to reuse them quickly, you need to remove the hot cookies to a rack (unlike parchment, which allows you to leave the cookies on it) and then wash the silicone mats in cool water and dry them. This special treatment plus the fact that they cost a minimum of about 18 dollars apiece have led us to prefer the conve-nience of parchment for cookie baking.

✳ **COOLING RACKS.** The purpose of a cooling rack is to allow air circulation underneath cookies for efficient cooling. Ours do double-duty as surfaces for drying our decorated cookies as well, and we recommend you own at least a couple. There are different types of racks. The widely available wire-grid type allows you the options of cooling the cookies directly on the rack or setting the hot cookie sheet directly on the grid until the whole pan is cool. For space-challenged frequent cookie makers, there are racks that stack cookie-condo style. Our favorite model stacks cookie sheets four high and folds to a mere

1 inch in width for storage. It requires you to leave the cookies on the sheets while they're cooling, however, so it's best for cookie crafters who have cookie sheets to spare. (See the box on page 76, for tips on cooling your cookies.)

* **METAL SPATULAS AND PANCAKE TURNERS.** Their thin blades are indispensable for a number of tasks. Small, narrow, offset blades (about 4 inches long by ¾ inch wide) are handy for removing excess dough from around unbaked cookies. Larger and wider offsets are good for removing cookies from cookie sheets. Thin, wide metal pancake turners are great for moving cookies (especially fragile shapes) without breaking them or without disturbing the icing on still-drying cookies.

* **TWO-CUP AIRTIGHT PLASTIC CONTAINERS.** We use these to mix icing colors — one for each outline color and one for each flood color. The airtight lids keep the icing from drying out while we're working, and we have enough on hand that we don't have to wash them in the middle of the process.

* **PASTRY BAGS.** Disposable pastry bags make clean-up much easier; they're our bags of choice. Ateco and Wilton make 12-inch disposable bags that cost about 3 dollars for a package of twelve. Quart-sized zip-top freezer bags can be substituted for pastry bags in a pinch. (Be sure not to use thin sandwich bags; they don't hold up.) Pastry bags are most often used with pastry tips; we also highly recommend using couplers (see below) to make changing tips easy (see chapter 6, page 102).

* **METAL DECORATING TIPS.** The most versatile decorating tip for cookie decorating is #2 (a thin, plain line). We use it to outline cookies that we will be flooding and to create most simple lines. Because tips are only 1 to 2 dollars apiece, it's a huge convenience to have a tip for every color, which saves having to change and clean tips frequently during decorating. Noted in the chart below are the tips we use most frequently, but there may be more you like to use. Experiment!

METAL DECORATING TIPS

SIZE	USE FOR
#00, #0, AND #1	EXTRA-THIN LINES, WRITING (ESPECIALLY IN BLACK)
#2	ALL-PURPOSE LINE
#4	WIDER LINES, OUTLINING IF ICING IS A BIT STIFF
#45	WIDE BASKET WEAVE (GOOD FOR BASKETS, MUMMY'S BANDAGES, ETC.)
#46	BASKET WEAVE — HAS RIDGES TO CREATE TEXTURE
#67	LEAF TIP FOR LEAVES

* **COUPLERS.** These two-piece plastic doohickeys are great to have if you're going to change decorating tips to make different textures in the same color during your decorating. Because couplers are very inexpensive, we recommend that you buy a half dozen or so; you'll use one for each icing color and/or pastry bag.

* **TWIST TIES.** Since the advent of the zip-top bag, these have become a rare commodity, but we find them essential when using pastry bags. (See chapter 6, page 103, for how to use them with pastry bags.) A word of advice: Hoard them when you have them, and reuse!

* **TIP BRUSH.** One end of this little tool is a mini bottle brush that's great for cleaning your decorating tips. The other end is a flat brush, like a small, stiff paintbrush. You can also use pipe cleaners or toothpicks to clean your tips.

* **SQUEEZE BOTTLES.** Using a 6-inch squeeze bottle is the easiest way we've found to apply flood icing.

* **PASTRY BRUSH.** The 1-inch-wide size is helpful if you're working with corn syrup. Use it to spread corn syrup "glue" on the cookies so that fondant will adhere or to apply corn syrup to a naked cookie after baking so that sugar will stick to it. A brush is also useful for sweeping excess sugar off cookie designs.

* **X-ACTO KNIFE.** This razor-sharp, narrow blade is perfect for cutting out templates and cutting cookie dough from templates.

* **SMALL PAINTBRUSHES.** Use small, cheap kids' paintbrushes to apply luster dust or egg tempera. Make sure that these are clean and reserved only for food-safe uses.

* **TWEEZERS.** Buy a pair of tweezers to help precisely place dragees or other sugar add-ons; keep them with your other decorating supplies and use them only for food.

Adding a pearl
dragee could be fun

Cut hole with
straw before baking

Pipe with lines
dots tiles coul
be fun

simple and white
wet floo...
try rolled fondant

cookie craft planning

A little forethought can save a lot of time and energy — and can help you avoid wasted effort. Here we've listed some reminders for you and have included the organizational hints and tips we've acquired along the way.

You might already know the information here, or you might like to wing it. But if you've never decorated cookies before or you want to make more complex cookies than you have in the past, read through this chapter so you don't make any of the mistakes we made when we were starting out — such as learning too late that we forgot to make one of our icing colors or not leaving enough time for the cookies to dry before we wrapped them. Oops.

plan your cookies before you bake

If you're creating elaborate or multistage showstopper cookies, there are a number of decisions to make before you begin baking and decorating, all of which will impact the look of your finished cookie design. These can include, for example, the flavor and color of the dough you'll be using for your cookie background and the colors of icing you'll need to execute your design. We suggest you jot down your plans. Following are the factors to think about ahead of time.

DESIGN YOUR COOKIES

Ever look at a cookie cutter and think, "How the heck do I fill in that shape?" So do we! Planning starts with your design. There's a wealth of inspiration here in *Cookie Craft,* and we encourage you to design your own cookies as well.

To make your own design, start by tracing the shape of the cookie cutter onto a piece of paper. This will allow you to sketch your design in colored pencil, crayon, or marker to provide a guide for your decorating. If you're at a loss for how to design a specific shape, we suggest using an Internet search engine to locate images of what you'd like to copy. This is how we got the ideas for our astronaut's spacesuit (page 43). Don't forget that you can use simple shapes to create a variety of designs. For instance, circles can become an Easter basket (page 15) or a cute baby's bib (page 41).

If you're just having fun, bake and go wild! But if you have a specific cookie goals — special designs, gift-sending — here's a chart with some questions that are good to answer before you begin.

cookie craft plan

Use this planning list as you prepare for your cookie-making session; you can even photocopy it. Refer to your cookie sketches or the *Cookie Craft* inspirations to make sure you have everything you need.

Cookie type(s) (sugar, chocolate, nutty, gingerbread)

_____

_____

Flavorings (for sugar cookies; citrus zest or extract)

_____

_____

Dough coloring (for sugar cookies)

_____

Desired number and approximate size of finished cookies (to help determine how many batches of dough you'll have to make)

_____

Cookies shapes (if you're shipping cookies, see chapter 8 for hints about shapes)

_____

_____

Prebaking decorating techniques (imprinting, making holes, making windowpanes, layering cookies, egg-tempera painting, sugaring, attaching add-ons)

_____

_____

Prebaking equipment and ingredients (implements for imprinting, colors of sugar)

_____

_____

After-baking decorating techniques (piping, flooding, feathering, attaching add-ons, sugaring, adding luster dust, using marking pens, using fondant)

_____

_____

After-baking equipment and ingredients (number of pastry bags and tips, luster dust colors, etc.)

_____

_____

Master list of icing colors (see Plan Icing Palettes, page 66)

_____

_____

Drying time for royal icing (NOTE: If you're adding multiple layers of royal icing, you'll need drying time between layers — especially important to consider when making showstoppers)

_____

Whether you're shipping or hand-delivering

_____

Wrappers, containers, packing materials, shipping boxes

_____

Shipping method and delivery time required (see chapter 8)

_____

PLAN ICING PALETTES

If you're making cookies in specific designs, it's helpful to write out the colors and types of icings required for each different cookie. From this information, you can make a master list of icing colors you'll need. This is especially important if you're following multiple cookie designs — nothing is more frustrating than coloring your icings and then realizing you forgot a color that's necessary for a small detail. Keep your design illustrations handy and refer to them when making the complete list of colors you'll need.

As an example, here are our individual palette lists for snowman and turkey cookies, as well as a master list for icings for both cookies. We check off each color on the individual list as we include it on the master. Then we double-check to be sure all colors are included!

SNOWMAN

COOKIE ELEMENT	OUTLINE (PIPING) COLOR	FLOOD COLOR
BODY	WHITE	WHITE
SCARF	BLUE	BLUE
HAT	BLACK	BLACK
EYES	BLUE	
MOUTH	RED	

TURKEY

COOKIE ELEMENT	OUTLINE (PIPING) COLOR	FLOOD COLOR
BODY	BLACK	BLACK
FEATHERS 1		ORANGE
FEATHERS 2		BLUE
WATTLE	ORANGE	
EYE	BLACK, ORANGE	
FOOT	ORANGE	

MASTER LIST OF COLORS NEEDED

OUTLINE (PIPING) COLOR	FLOOD COLOR
WHITE	WHITE
RED	ORANGE
BLACK	BLACK
BLUE	BLUE
ORANGE	

IN COOKIES AS IN LIFE,

ALWAYS THINK "JUST IN CASE"

Even if white is not on your master list of required colors for a cookie-decorating session, it's handy to leave a little uncolored (white) piping and flood icing just in case you need to mix up more of a color or you have a last-minute inspiration that calls for an unplanned color. Make sure to keep this extra icing in a lidded airtight container.

SOME SUGGESTED
COLOR PALETTES

If you're new to cookie decorating or you're creating a batch just for fun, we find that it's best to start with four colors. This means you have to mix eight colors in all (four piping colors and four matching flood colors). Of course, you should feel free to experiment or to follow the colors shown on our chapter 1 cookies, but the chart below includes the most common colors for the specified occasions.

OCCASION	COLOR 1	COLOR 2	COLOR 3	COLOR 4	OPTION
HALLOWEEN	orange	black	yellow	brown	white
THANKSGIVING	brown	red	orange	yellow	green
CHRISTMAS	green	red	black	white	gold
HANUKKAH	blue	yellow	white		silver
NEW YEAR'S	black	white	beige	silver	gold
VALENTINE'S DAY	red	pink	white		
EASTER/SPRING	pastel purple	pastel pink	pastel yellow	white	pastel blue
WEDDING	white	silver			wedding theme color
BABY	pastel blue	pastel pink	pastel yellow	white	pastel purple
FOURTH OF JULY	red	white	blue	black	

organize your baking

Unless we're baking cookies purely for the whole lovely experience — as we do to preserve holiday traditions or with children or friends — we've learned to break down the process into steps and to do as much ahead of time as possible.

TIME-SAVING MEASURES

Baking in advance makes for a more fun and focused decorating session. Undecorated cookies freeze well, so we bake a batch whenever we can squeeze in a spare hour or two. This is especially helpful in the peak cookie crunch time before the fall and winter holidays. (See chapter 8, page 134, for tips on how to successfully freeze cookies and even unbaked dough.)

Janice prefers mixing the dry ingredients as she goes. Valerie has to move half a dozen pantry items to get at the canisters in her tiny Manhattan kitchen, so, while she has the flour and sugar out, she mixes several batches of dry ingredients (flour, salt, cocoa, spices, espresso powder, and so on.) and measures out her sugar separately, then stores them for later use in airtight plastic containers or even zip-top bags. If this mix-ahead method appeals to you, simply dump the dry ingredients in your chosen containers, cover or zip them, and shake them vigorously to mix. Don't forget to label the containers with ingredients and the date — it's amazing how quickly we forget! When you're ready to bake, simply follow the recipe and add the dry ingredients when they're called for.

On the facing page is a handy chart that gives more make-ahead tips as well as estimated times for each step in the cookie-making process.

MAKE-AHEAD TIPS

STEP	TIME REQUIRED	TIME-SAVING MEASURES
SOFTENING BUTTER	approximately ½–1 hour (inactive time)	Take the butter out of the refrigerator about an hour before you're going to use it. Make sure it's well wrapped or covered and keep it clear of any warm appliances that might melt it. Cutting the butter into smaller pieces speeds up the softening process. To speed it even further, you can beat it with your stand mixer (using the paddle attachment), but make sure it's soft and creamy before you add the sugar.
MEASURING DRY INGREDIENTS	5 minutes, but you have to clean up afterward, so why not mix a couple of batches at the same time?	Measure and mix dry ingredients (excluding sugar) in an airtight container; shake to mix. Measure and store sugar separately in an airtight container. All dry ingredients keep indefinitely in a cool, dry place. Label containers with contents.
MIXING	10 minutes	You can mix cookie dough up to three days ahead and refrigerate it. Take it out and allow it to soften before rolling it. You can freeze dough in flattened disks for up to two months (see page 134). Thaw the frozen dough overnight in the refrigerator.
ROLLING AND CUTTING DOUGH	1–1½ hours (beginners); 30–45 minutes (with practice)	Cut-out cookies can be frozen and then baked later without being thawed (see page 134).
BAKING	12–16 minutes per cookie sheet; generally 45 minutes per batch of dough	You can freeze just-baked cookies for up to three months.
COOLING	45–60 minutes (inactive time)	No real shortcuts here. Cookies must cool completely before you can decorate them with icing.
TOTAL OF ACTIVE COOKIE-MAKING TIME	2½–3 hours (beginners); 2 hours (with practice)	It doesn't take much longer to make two batches than it does to make one.

organize your decorating

Begin by gathering all the items you will need to make your cookie-decorating session productive, efficient, and fun. Having all your materials at the ready before you start decorating will ensure uninterrupted creative flow!

decorating supplies checklist

Plastic tablecloths to cover your work area. (Trust us; you'll be glad you have these.)

Pint glasses or similar tall, stable containers (ideally, one for each color icing).

Clean, damp sponges or wet paper towels to place at the bottoms of the pint glasses. (These keep the icing tips moist.)

Plenty of toothpicks.

A bowl of water.

Sturdy paper plates. (These are handy for group decorating.)

Sanitary hand wipes. (These are great to have on your decorating table — especially after you've accidentally licked your fingers! You'll be especially happy to have them when you're decorating with children.)

Drying surfaces. (Rimmed cookie sheets and racks are ideal.)

Unbaked cookies (for prebaking decoration) and/or **baked and completely cooled cookies** (for after-baking decoration).

Pastry bags (fitted with desired tips) filled with piping icing in desired colors.

Squeeze bottles filled with flood icing in desired colors.

Decorating implements, depending on the techniques you're using: straws, mini cookie or aspic cutters, imprinting implements, tweezers, pastry brushes, and so forth.

Prebaking and after-baking add-ons, depending on the techniques and designs you're using: sugars, dragees, paillettes, confetti shapes, fondant, corn syrup, and so forth.

ORGANIZE YOUR WORK AREA

When setting up your equipment and supplies for maximum decorating efficiency and ease, here are some points to keep in mind.

* In general — and especially if decorating involves more than one person — the decorating supplies such as icings and add-ons should go in the middle of the table, within easy reach of everyone. The same goes for equipment that everyone needs (toothpicks, sanitary hand wipes, and so forth).

* We prefer to decorate the cookies on the same type of sheets we use for baking. Set up your cookie decorating surfaces (for example, baking sheets) around the perimeter of the table and arrange them so that iced cookies won't have to be moved before the icing has set. This means the decorators, not the cookies, will be moving around the table!

* Set up additional "safe" drying areas away from the main decorating table. About an hour after being iced, the cookies will be set enough that you can move the trays carefully out of the way to another drying spot.

An organized decorating area

DECORATING TIME ESTIMATES		
STEP	TIME REQUIRED	TIME-SAVING MEASURE
MIXING AND COLORING ICING	45–60 minutes per recipe, depending on the number of colors mixed	We prefer to make and color icing just before we use it, but you can make it a day ahead (see chapter 6, page 100, for extensive facts about icing properties).
DECORATING COOKIES	1–2 hours for prebaking techniques, which tend to go more quickly than royal icing sessions; 2–3 hours for decorating a full batch of cookies with royal icing; 1 hour for decorating with children, using any method.	
LETTING THE ICING DRY	If you're flooding cookies and you're planning wet-on-dry-flood decoration, wait at least 2 hours for each flooded layer. Depending on the humidity and desired effects, you may have to wait as long as overnight. If you're packing and shipping cookies (see chapter 8), overnight drying — or more — is essential.	Drying time varies with icing consistency. As with nail polish, the more coats of icing, the longer the cookie takes to dry completely.

IF YOU HAVE PETS

Move any chairs far away from the decorating table and drying area to deny Rover or Snowball easy access to cookies. However, we know from experience that this method is not guaranteed! Therefore, mesh food tents (used to protect picnic food from bugs) are great for preventing unwanted pet hair from landing on cookies while they're drying. They're available in a range of sizes and cost anywhere from 2 to 10 dollars. Best of all, they fold up like umbrellas to take up minimal storage space when they're not in use. You can find them at a number of the Internet retailers listed in the resources.

If you're decorating a sizable quantity of the same cookie, adopt an assembly-line mind-set: Decorating will go faster if you complete one feature at a time on all the cookies before you proceed to the next detail. For example, on the cat on page 47, imprint the features first, then go back and add all the dragree necklaces.

When piping and flooding, first pipe the outlines on all the cookies before you begin flooding. On Christmas trees, for example, outline all the yellow stars, then outline the green bodies of the trees. Then start flooding one color at a time, in the same assembly-line fashion.

DECORATING CLEANUP

The good news is that decorating cleanup is actually easier than it looks. Icing is mostly sugar, after all, and, like the Wicked Witch of the West, it melts away with water.

Fill a dishpan with the-hotter-the-better soapy water and throw your cookie cutters in. Snip the tips and couplers from the pastry bags and cut the excess plastic from them. Don't forget to save your twist ties!

Throw the couplers into the hot, soapy water. Throw out the bags and leftover icing. Use a toothpick or a small brush to remove all the icing from the tips (if you've let your tips sit for a while, the icing will have dried out and you might have to soak them a bit), and add the tips to the soapy water. For efficient rinsing (and to prevent losing any tips), dump your cookie cutters and tips into a colander and thoroughly douse them with piping hot water.

cookie recipes for creating blank canvases

At the heart of the best cookie craft creations is a tasty cookie, rolled to an

even thickness and baked to perfection. In this chapter, we'll show you how

to create the blank canvases for your cookie masterpieces. If you're new to

cookie crafting or want to make complex cookies, check out chapter 3, Cookie

Craft Planning, for hints on how to plan your baking (choose shapes, plan

dough colors) and decorating (making icing colors) so that the process is as

smooth as it is fun.

basic recipes and methods

We've developed our cookie recipes to be delicious as well as to provide a perfect decorating surface, but if you've mastered your grandma's favorite rolled-cookie recipe and she'll disown you if you start baking someone else's, feel free to use hers. We understand.

Whatever recipe you decide to use, before you prepare your dough for baking, refer to Ready to Roll on page 83 for methods and tips for making uniform cookies quickly and with a minimum of mess. These methods changed our cookie-baking lives!

If you don't have a favorite rolled-cookie recipe, try any of those that follow, and note that recipe yields are necessarily approximate because cookie shapes vary so much.

IN COOKIES AS IN LIFE, **IT'S BETTER TO COOL OFF FAST**

Your cookies will cool slightly faster if they're taken off the hot cookie sheets and placed directly on the cooling rack. With the parchment method described in Ready to Roll (page 83), however, there's no danger of your cookies sticking once they've cooled. You can either (carefully) slide the whole parchment sheet full of cookies right onto the rack or you can remove the cookies one by one with a thin spatula and place them on the rack to cool without parchment.

Both of these methods give you the benefit of being able to reuse the cookie sheet quickly – just rinse it in cold water to cool it, and then dry it. If you have plenty of cookie sheets, though, you can place the pan right on the cooling rack with no adverse effects. In a pinch, you could even place a stove burner or a raised trivet on any cool, flat surface (i.e., not on your warm stove!) and rest the cookie sheet on top of it.

ROLLED SUGAR COOKIES

We especially like to add lemon zest to give these a fresh zing, but they're tasty with vanilla alone.

yield

2½-inch cookies — about 30

3½-inch cookies — about 16

4½-inch cookies — about 12

ingredients

3 cups all-purpose flour

½ teaspoon salt

1 cup (2 sticks) unsalted butter, softened

1 cup sugar

1 large egg

2 teaspoons vanilla* or 1 teaspoon vanilla plus zest of 1 lemon

food coloring (if your cookie design calls for it)

* *Instead of vanilla, you can use other extracts such as almond or peppermint, which we like for candy-cane shapes. If you're going to be decorating with royal icing, make sure the cookie and icing flavorings are complementary.*

1 Whisk together the flour and salt in a medium bowl and set aside.

2 Using your mixer, cream together the butter and sugar until the mixture is light and fluffy. (If your mixer has multiple attachments, use the paddle.) Add the egg and vanilla (and lemon zest, if you're using it) or your extract of choice and mix until well blended.

3 With the mixer on low, gradually add the flour mixture to the butter mixture until the two are thoroughly blended.

4 If your cookie design calls for adding food coloring, do so now, and continue blending until the desired color is reached and is evenly incorporated. (For tips on coloring, see Coloring Dough, page 78.)

5 Turn out the dough onto the work surface and divide it into two or three equal portions. Form each one into a rough disk. Now you're ready to roll, chill, and cut out the cookie shapes. Find complete rolling and cutting instructions under Ready to Roll on page 83.

6 Preheat the oven to 350°F.

7 After you've rolled and cut the dough and the cookie shapes are on parchment-lined cookie sheets, bake them in the middle rack of your oven for 12–16 minutes or until the cookies start to turn slightly golden around the edges (smaller cookies will be done more quickly). **NOTE:** If you decide to bake two sheets of cookies at a time, space your two oven racks evenly in the oven and rotate the cookie sheets halfway through baking (that is, switch the position of the top sheet and bottom sheet and turn both so that the front of each sheet is at the back to promote even baking).

8 Cool the cookies completely on a rack before icing or decorating (see the box at left, for cooling hints).

COLORING DOUGH

Your cookie design may call for coloring the dough. Generally speaking, super-market coloring will yield a hint of color; gels will yield more saturated, vibrant colors. We like softer colors on fall-tone cookies, where a hint is all you need; more vibrancy is fun for greens, like the Father's Day putting green. For supermarket colors, use the color chart on page 52 as your guide. For both liquids and gels, add just a couple of drops at a time — you can always add more.

cookie recipes for creating blank canvases

ROLLED CHOCOLATE COOKIES

The deep, rich color of this dough makes for great spooky Halloween shapes. They're also great for Valentine's Day hearts — in fact, some people believe chocolate to be an aphrodisiac — or any time you desire a chocolate-flavored cookie or a darker background for your decorative genius.

yield

2½-inch cookies — about 30
3½-inch cookies — about 16
4½-inch cookies — about 12

ingredients

2½ cups all-purpose flour
½ cup cocoa powder, either alkalized (Dutch-process) or natural (non-alkalized)
1 teaspoon instant espresso powder (optional but recommended)
½ teaspoon salt
1 cup (2 sticks) unsalted butter, softened
1 cup sugar
1 large egg
1 teaspoon vanilla

1 Whisk together the flour, cocoa powder, espresso powder, and salt in a medium bowl and set aside.

2 Using your mixer, cream together the butter and sugar until the mixture is light and fluffy. (If your mixer has multiple attachments, use the paddle.) Add the egg and vanilla and mix until well blended.

3 With the mixer on low, gradually add the flour mixture to the butter mixture until the two are thoroughly blended.

4 Turn out the dough onto the work surface and divide it into two or three equal portions. Form each one into a rough disk. Now you're ready to roll, chill, and cut out the cookie shapes. Find complete rolling and cutting instructions under Ready to Roll on page 83.

5 Preheat the oven to 350°F.

6 After you've rolled and cut the dough and the cookie shapes are on parchment-lined cookie sheets, bake in the middle rack of your oven for 12–16 minutes or until the cookies start to turn a deeper brown around the edges (smaller cookies will be done more quickly).
NOTE: If you decide to bake two sheets of cookies at a time, space your two oven racks evenly in the oven and rotate the cookie sheets halfway through baking (that is, switch the position of the top sheet and bottom sheet and turn both so that the front of each sheet is at the back to promote even baking).

7 Cool the cookies completely on a rack before icing or decorating (for cooling hints, see the box on page 76).

These exceptionally flavorful cookies have been a hit with everyone who's tried them. They also have an interesting color and texture; we particularly like them for our Thanksgiving turkeys and other autumn cookie creations.

yield

2½-inch cookies — about 30
3½-inch cookies — about 16
4½-inch cookies — about 12

ingredients

1 cup nuts of choice,* toasted and ground as directed
3 cups all-purpose flour
½ teaspoon salt
1 cup (2 sticks) unsalted butter, softened
1 cup sugar
1 large egg
2 teaspoons vanilla

* *Pecans are our favorite nuts to use in baking cookies, but walnuts and almonds are also good.*

1 Place the nuts on a cookie sheet and bake in a 350° oven until they're fragrant and light brown, about 10 minutes. Watch carefully; they go from perfect to burned very quickly. (We know this from experience!) When you start to smell them, they're done. Let cool.

2 Whisk together the flour and salt in a medium bowl and set aside.

3 In your food processor, pulse together the cooled nuts plus 2 or 3 tablespoons of the flour/salt mixture. Continue pulsing until the nuts are finely ground and have a texture like that of wet sand, making sure there are no large nut pieces (which might disrupt the smooth surface of your finished cookie). Be sure not to overprocess the mixture or you'll end up with nut butter!

4 Add the nut mixture to the remaining flour mixture and whisk together to blend well.

5 Using your mixer, cream together the butter and sugar until the mixture is light and fluffy. (If your mixer has multiple attachments, use the paddle.) Add the egg and vanilla and mix until well blended.

6 With the mixer on low, gradually add the flour and nut mixture to the butter mixture until the two are thoroughly blended.

7 Turn out the dough onto the work surface and divide it into two or three equal portions. Form each one into a rough disk. Now you're ready to roll, chill, and cut out the cookie shapes. Find complete rolling and cutting instructions under Ready to Roll on page 83.

8 Preheat the oven to 350°F.

**SOMETIMES YOU MAKE
DOUGH NOW
AND USE IT LATER**

*If you're not going to roll your
cookies immediately after making
the dough, wrap each disk
in plastic wrap and refrigerate.
(It can also be frozen at
this point; see Freezing Unbaked
Cookie Dough, on page 134.)
If the dough is refrigerated for
more than 2 hours, before
attempting to roll it, let it sit at
room temperature until it's
pliable enough to roll, at least
30 minutes.*

9 After you've rolled and cut the dough and the cookie shapes are on parchment-lined cookie sheets, bake in the middle rack of your oven for 12–16 minutes or until the cookies start to turn barely golden around the edges (smaller cookies will be done more quickly).

NOTE: If you decide to bake two sheets of cookies at a time, space your two oven racks evenly in the oven and rotate the cookie sheets halfway through baking (that is, switch the position of the top sheet and bottom sheet and turn both so that the front of each sheet is at the back to promote even baking).

10 Cool the cookies completely on a rack before icing or decorating (for cooling hints, see the box on page 76).

ROLLED GINGERBREAD COOKIES

These cookies have a mild gingerbread flavor, and they make the kitchen smell wonderful while they're baking! Feel free to increase the spices or even add the zest of an orange if you like. Note that this recipe yields more than the others: One recipe makes enough for the Santa's sleigh centerpiece on page 127.

yield

2½-inch cookies — about 48
3-inch cookies — about 37
4½-inch cookies — about 18

ingredients

5 cups all-purpose flour
2 teaspoons ground ginger
1 teaspoon ground cinnamon
1 teaspoon ground cloves
½ teaspoon baking soda*
½ teaspoon salt
zest of one orange (optional)
1 cup (2 sticks) unsalted butter,
   softened
1 cup granulated sugar
1 large egg
1 cup molasses

* Omit baking soda if baking for cookie construction; see Baking Cookies for Construction on
  page 129.

1 Whisk together the flour, ginger, cinnamon, cloves, baking soda, salt, and orange zest (if using) in a medium bowl and set aside.

2 Using your mixer, cream together the butter and sugar until the mixture is light and fluffy. (If your mixer has multiple attachments, use the paddle.) Add the egg and molasses and mix until well blended.

3 With the mixer on low, gradually add the flour mixture to the butter mixture until the two are thoroughly blended.

4 Turn out the dough onto the work surface and divide it into three equal portions. Form each one into a rough disk. Now you're ready to roll, chill, and cut out the cookie shapes. Find complete rolling and cutting instructions under Ready to Roll on the facing page.

5 Preheat the oven to 350°F.

6 After you've rolled and cut the dough and the cookie shapes are on parchment-lined cookie sheets, bake in the middle rack of your oven for 12–16 minutes or until the cookies start to turn slightly darker around the edges (smaller cookies will be done more quickly).
   NOTE: If you decide to bake two sheets of cookies at a time, space your two oven racks evenly in the oven and rotate the cookie sheets halfway through baking (that is, switch the position of the top sheet and bottom sheet and turn both so that the front of each sheet is at the back to promote even baking).

7 Cool the cookies completely on a rack before icing or decorating (for cooling hints, see the box on page 76).

READY TO ROLL: ROLLING, CUTTING, AND BAKING DOUGH

We both made cookies the hard way, with lots of flour and no helpful tools, until, little by little, we discovered ways to make the rolling and cutting process easier. One of our favorites — and the only method we use now — is to roll out the dough between wax paper or parchment before it's chilled. This method has many advantages: The rolled dough chills quickly for cutting, and you don't need to use extra flour to prevent sticking in the rolling process (it won't stick to the wax paper or parchment), so your dough doesn't get dry. Your last roll-out and cutting of the dough is as good as your first, and you won't waste even a smidge of dough.

Any smooth kitchen surface will do for rolling cookies — laminate or solid-surface countertops, marble, or wood.

1 Place a cookie-sheet-sized piece of wax paper or parchment on your rolling surface. If you use parchment underneath your rolled dough, when you cut cookies from the chilled dough, you can directly transfer the parchment and the cut cookies to a cookie sheet — you won't need to carefully transfer each cookie. Just make sure to cut out cookies in approximately the same size and leave ½ inch between cookies when you cut them out (see step 6).

2 Place ¼-inch cookie slats on the edges of the paper. The slats should be rolling-pin-width apart, to ensure that there's stable contact between the slats and both ends of the rolling pin.

3 Place a disk of cookie dough on top of the paper, between the slats. Place a sheet of wax paper over the cookie dough and slats and use your hand or rolling pin to slightly flatten and evenly distribute the dough across the paper. Roll the pin over the paper-covered dough, making sure the ends of the pin stay on the slats as the dough flattens (the pin will hover above the slats at first).

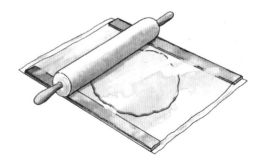

Using slats to roll out dough

If the top paper wrinkles, lift and smooth it. You're finished rolling when the dough surface is uniform and completely level with the cookie slats. At this point, you'll feel that rolling the pin over the dough is effortless. Because the dough is soft, this will happen quickly.

4   Slide the rolled-out piece of dough (paper and all) onto a cookie sheet and refrigerate it until it's firm (this should take 20–30 minutes). Repeat the rolling process with the remaining dough portions.

5   When the dough is firm (it will pretty much be stiff as a board), remove it from the refrigerator to your flat work surface. Work with one piece of dough at a time, leaving the others to chill in the refrigerator until you're ready to cut them. Peel back the top paper from the dough and cut the dough into the desired shapes. Don't worry about the direction of the cookies in the dough as you're cutting; the goal is to get as many cookies as possible out of each rolled-out piece of dough.

6   Remove excess dough from around the shapes (a small, narrow offset spatula comes in handy for this task). If you've used parchment on the bottom of the dough, you can transfer the parchment, cookies and all, directly to a cookie sheet for baking. If you've rolled on wax paper, carefully use a thin metal spatula or pancake turner to transfer the cookies from the wax paper to your parchment-lined cookie sheet, leaving ½ inch between cookies (cookies from our recipes don't spread much in the oven). It's best to keep cookies of the same size together on a sheet for uniform baking — remember that

Cutting cookies

Trimming excess dough

Transferring dough to prepared baking sheets

different sizes of cookies will be done at different times.

If the dough is too sticky to allow you to move the cookies without stretching or tearing them, slide the dough — still on the wax paper — onto a cookie sheet and put it back in the refrigerator for a few minutes until the dough is firm, and then continue.

When you've cut as many cookies as possible from your first rolled piece, gather the dough scraps into a ball and roll it again, using the same rolling method. Continue to cut cookies and reroll the dough until you've used all the dough, chilling the rolled dough whenever it becomes too sticky to work with.

7 If you're using any of the prebaking decorating methods (impressing, sugaring, add-ons, and so on), now's the time to get decorating. See chapter 5 for a wealth of prebaking decorating techniques.

8 Bake and cool the cookies as directed in the individual recipes.

WHAT TO DO WITH IRREGULARS

Don't throw out your broken or uneven cookies! Remember: Icing covers a host of mistakes, or you can use irregular cookies to practice piping designs or to test colors. . . . Or you could always eat them! We toss burned cookies, however; they just don't taste right.

IN COOKIES AS IN LIFE,
SOMETIMES YOU HAVE TO DO WITHOUT

We've sung the praises of wax paper and parchment paper and cookie slats for good reason, but, of course, you can work without them. If you're "going commando" without paper or slats, follow these rolling methods.

   ✳ *If you have no wax paper or parchment, lightly but thoroughly dust flour on your rolling surface and your rolling pin, follow the cutting method outlined in steps 5 and 6, and be sure to dust the flour off the cookies before baking them (a pastry brush is handy for this). Be aware that as the dough absorbs the excess flour, any leftover dough that you roll again will be drier, and it may become mottled in appearance and crack.*

   ✳ *If you don't have cookie slats, get out your handy ruler, a toothpick, and a sharp pencil. Roll out the dough until it looks even to your eye. Measure the thickness at the edges of your dough – get as close as possible to ¼ inch. To measure to see if the dough is even all the way across, stick a toothpick in the center of the rolled dough, mark the toothpick with the pencil where the top of the dough hits it, then measure the depth on the toothpick. Proceed with cutting the cookies once your measurement is ¼ inch.*

5

prebaking decorating techniques

The cookie crafter's repertoire should include the gamut of easy, versatile prebaking decorating techniques. From imprinting and add-ons that give cookies dimension to windowpanes, egg tempera, and sugar add-ons that lend color and interest, these techniques can be used in combination with royal icing or by themselves to create beautiful, whimsical, or just plain fun cookie designs. Once you've mastered the techniques, you are limited only by your imagination! Before decorating your cookies, take a few minutes to peruse chapter 3, Cookie Craft Planning, for hints on how to make the process smoother and more successful.

IMPRINTING AN UNBAKED COOKIE

Imprinting your cookie dough before baking — that is, pressing designs into the raw dough — creates visual interest or highlights cookie features. We've used our spatulas, toothpicks, drinking straws, and a variety of other household items to create particular imprinted shapes. For example, you can use the side of a flat toothpick to mark an acorn's cap or the blade of a small knife to imprint lines on a bat's wings. Look around your house for objects that can make interesting impressions on your cookies. Imprinting in combination with other techniques — such as adding luster dust or using sugar add-ons — increases the cookies' level of detail.

Imprinting bat wing details

CREATING WINDOWPANES

Windowpanes create a see-through glass effect on cookies. They're often used on Christmas cookies to create a look of stained glass, but we've also used them for the windows on our Halloween haunted house luminaria (page 122). To create windowpanes:

1 Make holes of the desired sizes and shapes in the unbaked cookies (we've had the best results with holes at least ½ inch in diameter).

2 Place hard candies in a double-layer zip-top freezer bag and crush them with a hammer or hard mallet until they're powdery or in tiny shards.

3 Completely fill the holes in the unbaked cookies with crushed candy. The candy should be at least even with the top of the dough or piled a little higher — it will recede as it melts. For neatest results, brush excess candy from the raw cookie around the hole with a pastry brush.

4 During baking, the candy melts to create the windowpane.

5 Be sure not to remove the cookies from the cookie sheet until they've cooled completely and the candy has hardened again. Moving them too soon will cause a candy mess and ruin the cookies!

Crushing hard candies

Filling cookie hole with crushed candy

MAKING HOLES OR CUTOUTS

Perforating your cookies before baking is a deceptively simple technique that creates striking results. Holes or cutouts can be useful (for "stringing" an ornament cookie, adding handles to a shopping-bag cookie, or cutting out names on a place-card cookie), playful (round holes for a ghost's eyes or for the golf-ball hole on a putting green), or simply beautiful (hearts cutouts on a bridesmaid's-dress cookie). You can use a plastic drinking straw to create many designs. In addition, sets of tiny aspic cutters come in shapes that broaden your "hole" design options, as in the snowflake.

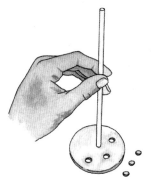

Making holes with a straw

ADDING DIMENSION TO COOKIES

You can add a second layer of dough detail to your base cookies to create dimension, such as the letters on a message cookie, the ornaments on a birthday crown, or the circles that make a turkey body. To achieve this effect, simply cut out the desired shapes and place them on top of the base cookie before baking. You can even mix and match doughs. These dimensional cookies generally take no more time to bake than single-layer cookies. **NOTE:** To create more complex dimension or to layer cookies that are fully iced (for example, cookie #8 on page 21, the piped-and-flooded jack-o'-lantern that extends beyond the edges of a piped-and-flooded tombstone), you can attach already-baked and already-decorated cookies with royal icing (see Multicookie Creations on page 116 in chapter 7 for instructions on this technique).

PAINTING WITH EGG TEMPERA AND USING EGG WASH

Made with an egg yolk and supermarket food coloring, tempera has been around since the earth cooled and creates an old-fashioned-looking, shiny painted surface.

1 Beat an egg yolk and divide it into separate small bowls, one for each desired color (one yolk can make up to three colors).

2 Add the food coloring to the yolks. Use a few drops to make saturated colors, but be aware that because you're mixing the very yellow egg yolk with the coloring, your final color is never going to be quite true to the original. (For example, blue will be a bit greenish.)

3 Although it's not mandatory, imprinting your unbaked cookies will create a natural border for your egg tempera colors.

4 Brush the tempera paint onto the unbaked cookie using a small, clean paintbrush and bake cookies as usual.

Adding egg wash is a simple technique that creates a shine on your cookie. To make an egg wash, beat a whole egg with a few drops of water and paint this on the unbaked cookie.

IN COOKIES AS IN LIFE, **TEST FIRST!**

When using candy add-ons of any kind, be sure to bake one test cookie before you bake a whole batch. Some candies withstand baking intact and some do not. If you haven't baked with a particular candy before, you might not know how it will hold up in the oven. For example, the colors may run or the candy may melt. Even two brands of the same candy may react differently to oven heat because different manufacturers use different ingredients.

Valerie learned this lesson the hard way: She used candy corn on cookies after baking and loved the effect. But when she added Indian candy corn to a turkey before baking, the candy bubbled up (it looked like the turkey had exploded!), then melted. The muted color effect wasn't bad, actually — but it wasn't what she had expected. Janice had a similar experience when she used red hots and the color ran.

SUGARING A COOKIE OR ATTACHING ADD-ONS

Sugaring a cookie adds color and sparkle and couldn't be simpler: Just sprinkle the sugar on unbaked cookies, making sure to fully cover the areas you want to sugar. To attach other add-ons — confetti, dragees, fruits, nuts, and so forth — place them on unbaked cookies and press firmly.

You can use stencils or cutters to create precise shapes with sugar. Cookie stencils are available from Wilton, but you can also use crafting or office stencils. You can even make your own with a piece of mylar and an X-acto knife. To sugar a cookie using a stencil, follow these steps.

1   Before using a stencil, use masking tape to block off any adjacent shapes on the stencil.

2   Spray or brush the stencil with a light coating of vegetable oil on the side that's going to be placed on the cookie. This creates a seal to prevent sugar from seeping beyond the stencil.

3   Sprinkle the sugar, then lift the stencil carefully to avoid marring the sugar design.

You can also use a small aspic cutter or cookie cutter as a guide for sugaring a specific shape onto a cookie. Place the cutter on the cookie and carefully sprinkle the sugar inside the cutter. To better direct your pour, you can fill a snack-sized zip-top bag with the sugar, snip off a small corner of the bag, and sprinkle from this.

Covering unused stencils with masking tape

Using cutters to create sugared shapes

after-baking decorating techniques

A cookie exquisitely decorated with royal icing is sure to impress — and even if your first tries are less than exquisite, the process is fun and creative.

In this chapter you'll find royal icing recipes, a variety of techniques to use with the icing, and a wealth of information and tips to help you master the process. It might take a little practice to get the results you want, but you'll have a good time doing it. Other after-baking decorating techniques, such as using rolled fondant and food-safe color markers, will add to your cookie craft repertoire. Whatever your after-baking decorating method, make sure your cookies have completely cooled before you start.

Once you've learned the basics of these techniques, you'll find loads of inspiration from the cookies pictured in this book and additional hints on planning your cookies and projects in chapter 3, Cookie Craft Planning.

ROYAL ICING RECIPES

Both of us admit to not always reading the entire recipe through before we start cooking. That said, if you've never made royal icing before, we *strongly* recommend that you read through the entire recipe and accompanying hints before you start. Once you've made royal icing, you'll see it's very easy — but because much depends on perfect icing consistency, and it's not an exact science, you'll want to understand the many variables (especially weather) and what you're looking for before you're in the middle of the process.

Each of these three royal icing recipes uses a different form of egg whites: powdered egg whites, liquid pasteurized egg whites, or meringue powder (see chapter 2 for a description of each). We don't recommend using fresh egg whites because of the risk of salmonella (an admittedly small risk, but why take chances?). Taste-wise, the recipes are largely indistinguishable from one another, and we've found they behave pretty much the same decoratively, as well.

To make any of them, first ensure that your bowls are spotless. Any amount of grease will prevent the icing from whipping properly.

Lemon juice is our favorite royal icing flavoring. Vanilla extract is another all-purpose flavoring that goes well with just about any cookie flavor — but it does give the icing a very slightly darker tinge. It's almost unnoticeable, but if you're looking for a bright white icing, use lemon juice or clear vanilla (available in specialty shops). If you do use traditional brown vanilla, you can add a bit of the gel color called "super white" to help counteract the slightly darker color.

Depending on what kind of cookie you're making, you can experiment with other extracts — for example, use peppermint icing on candy-cane cookies or almond icing on almond nutty cookies. Just make sure your icing flavor doesn't clash with your cookie flavor. Remember, too: Because each flavoring has its own strength, we recommend you add ½ teaspoon at a time so that you can adjust the icing flavor to your individual taste.

Although amounts will vary depending on your designs, in general you should plan to use a ½-pound recipe of piping royal icing and a 1-pound recipe of flood royal icing to pipe, flood, and detail two to three batches of rolled sugar cookies.

ROYAL ICING USING POWDERED EGG WHITES	CONFECTIONERS' SUGAR	POWDERED EGG WHITES	WARM WATER*	LEMON JUICE OR VANILLA OR OTHER EXTRACT
FOR PIPING	2 cups (½ pound)	1 teaspoon	3 tablespoons	1 tablespoon (lemon juice) or ½–1 teaspoon (extract)
	4 cups (1 pound)	2 teaspoons	6 tablespoons	2 tablespoons (lemon juice) or 1–2 teaspoons (extract)
FOR FLOODING	2 cups (½ pound)	1 teaspoon	6 tablespoons	1 tablespoon (lemon juice) or ½–1 teaspoon (extract)
	4 cups (1 pound)	2 teaspoons	12 tablespoons	2 tablespoons (lemon juice) or 1–2 teaspoons (extract)

*Starting amount; you may need to add more, especially if you use an extract rather than lemon juice.

ROYAL ICING USING LIQUID PASTEURIZED EGG WHITES	CONFECTIONERS' SUGAR	LIQUID PASTEURIZED EGG WHITES	WARM WATER*	LEMON JUICE OR VANILLA OR OTHER EXTRACT
FOR PIPING	2 cups (½ pound)	3 tablespoons	1 tablespoon	1 tablespoon (lemon juice) or ½–1 teaspoon (extract)
	4 cups (1 pound)	6 tablespoons	2 tablespoons	2 tablespoons (lemon juice) or 1–2 teaspoons (extract)
FOR FLOODING	2 cups (½ pound)	3 tablespoons	3 tablespoons	1 tablespoon (lemon juice) or ½–1 teaspoon (extract)
	4 cups (1 pound)	6 tablespoons	6 tablespoons	2 tablespoons (lemon juice) or 1–2 teaspoons (extract)

*Starting amount; you may need to add more, especially if you use an extract rather than lemon juice.

ROYAL ICING USING MERINGUE POWDER	CONFECTIONERS' SUGAR	MERINGUE POWDER	WARM WATER*	LEMON JUICE OR VANILLA OR OTHER EXTRACT
FOR PIPING	2 cups (½ pound)	4 teaspoons	3 tablespoons	1 tablespoon (lemon juice) or ½–1 teaspoon (extract)
	4 cups (1 pound)	3 tablespoons	6 tablespoons	2 tablespoons (lemon juice) or 1–2 teaspoons (extract)
FOR FLOODING	2 cups (½ pound)	4 teaspoons	6 tablespoons	1 tablespoon (lemon juice) or ½–1 teaspoon (extract)
	4 cups (1 pound)	3 tablespoons	12 tablespoons	2 tablespoons (lemon juice) or 1–2 teaspoons (extract)

*Starting amount; you may need to add more, especially if you use an extract rather than lemon juice.

❉ MAKING THE ROYAL ICING. The method is the same no matter what type of egg-white product you've used:

1 Combine all ingredients in the bowl of your electric mixer.

2 Beat on high for 5 minutes if you're using an electric stand mixer or for 10 minutes if you're using an electric hand mixer. (If your mixer has multiple attachments, use the paddle.)

3 When you reach the desired consistency, it's important that you immediately cover the mixture or store it in airtight containers, as instructed in Coloring and Keeping Icing (page 100).

Use the water amounts in our icing recipes as starting points, but be prepared to adjust them depending on the weather or even your kitchen temperature (for instance, when Valerie runs the dishwasher in her tiny Manhattan kitchen, the whole room gets very hot and humid). Be aware that the amount of water you add to icing may change slightly every time you make it.

Janice likes her outline icing on the thin side (so it blends seamlessly into the flood), but Valerie likes the control that comes with an outline of slightly thicker icing. The great news is that royal icing is very forgiving. We'll pass along to you all of our hints — and know that the more you work with royal icing, the more you'll figure out what your preference is and how to achieve it.

IN COOKIES AS IN LIFE,
MUCH DEPENDS ON THE WEATHER

Artful iced cookies depend largely on the consistency of the icing – and getting it right takes a little practice. Even though you might follow the icing recipe exactly, it never seems to come out the same way twice without some tweaking. Factors such as the humidity level, the temperature of your kitchen, and even your brand of confectioners' sugar can affect the outcome. We've noticed our icing comes out shinier in perfectly dry weather. The only way to learn what works is to roll up your sleeves and make it – and get comfortable adjusting the recipe so that it works for you.

PIPING CONSISTENCY SPECIFICS

⁂ When first mixed, piping icing will start out with the consistency of white glue. When you've finished beating the icing, it will be glossy with a consistency similar to that of toothpaste.

⁂ The icing should squeeze easily out of a #2 tip but should stay in place and hold its shape on the cookie when it lands.

⁂ If the icing is too stiff, it'll be hard to squeeze from the pastry bag and may lift up off the cookie when you finish the outline or detail. (It will also tend to "flake off" the cookie readily when dry.)

If the icing is too loose, it will spread and make too shallow an outline to dam the flood icing.

It's a good idea to test the icing consistency before you fill the pastry bags: Just put a small amount into the tip and, pushing it through with your thumb, make a practice loop or two on a piece of wax paper or your kitchen counter. Even though they might overlap, the loops should remain distinct rather than run together.

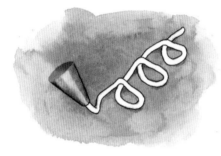

Testing icing consistency

FLOOD CONSISTENCY SPECIFICS

When first mixed, flood icing will appear very soupy. Never fear! In 5 minutes your icing will be shiny and an opaque white color with the consistency of heavy cream.

Flood icing is sometimes known as flow icing for a reason: When you squirt it onto a cookie, it immediately flows toward the piped borders.

This icing shouldn't be so thin that it runs like water or that its cookie coverage is transparent, and it shouldn't be so thick that it stays in place when you squirt it onto the cookie.

ICING CONSISTENCY

IF YOUR ICING IS TOO THICK:
Add water 1 teaspoon at a time and beat for 1 minute after each addition. Test the consistency and repeat until you get the results you want.

IF YOUR ICING IS TOO THIN:
Add more confectioners' sugar 1 tablespoon at a time and beat for 1 minute after each addition. Test the consistency and repeat until you get the results you want.

IF YOU NEED VERY STIFF ICING:
Occasionally, you might need to stiffen icing to maintain the distinct detail of your piping (for separate strands of hair or mummy bandages, for example). Start with the piping-consistency recipe and add confectioners' sugar 1 heaping tablespoon at a time, beating for 1 minute and testing the icing with each addition, until you can pipe the detail with no loss of distinction (i.e., the separate layers of icing don't meld together).

The more you practice, the more precisely you'll be able to predict the texture of your icing. But even if you're a beginner and your first efforts aren't perfect, your icing will be usable for decorating fun.

ABOUT MAKING ICING AHEAD OF TIME

*Royal icing starts changing texture just
a couple of hours after it's mixed; flood icing
separates, and piping icing loses its
smoothness and gets a little more watery. For best
results, make and color your icing just before using
it. If you really think you'll be pressed for
time and you need to do as much as possible ahead
of the decorating session, make the icing,
divide it among airtight containers, and store them
in the refrigerator (we recommend you do this
no earlier than the day before). When it's time to
decorate, make sure you mix the icings
thoroughly before coloring them. (To save even
more time, have your pastry bags set up and your
squeeze bottles ready to fill.)*

*If your colored flood icing has separated, you
can still use it; just mix it again before decorating
with it. Be aware, though, that separated
flood icing will create a mottled color effect on the
cookies. Though it's fine to use, for
picture-perfect cookies you may want to make fresh
icing. Piping icing that's been sitting in
a pastry bag may get a bit watery; again, it's fine
to use, but you may get unexpected drips or
pockets of loose icing, which make
for uneven piping.*

*You can store royal icing for up to three days
in the refrigerator and still get some decorating fun
out of it, but be aware that the texture
will deteriorate when it's stored.*

COLORING AND KEEPING ICING

Seeing our cookie craft palette come alive as we mix our icing colors is always a satisfying part of our decorating setup. The prelude to our creative session, it's a vibrant hint of the fun to come.

Even though it takes a while to fully dry on a cookie, royal icing dries out very quickly when you're working with it. Once your icing has reached the desired consistency, it's important to get it into airtight containers or cover it immediately. The easiest method is to put it right into the containers in which you'll be mixing your colors. We like containers with leak-proof, twist-on lids, but snap-on lids are fine, too. If you use small bowls, cover your icing with plastic wrap.

Use a separate container for each piping and flood color. Divide the icing into the containers, and tightly cover each.

Filling and covering icing containers

1   Work with one container at a time and keep the others tightly covered.

2   Add the desired food coloring to the icing. We suggest you add just a drop at a time, mixing well after each addition, until you achieve the desired color. Remember, you can always make a color deeper, but it's much harder to lighten it. Continue to mix well to ensure that the color is uniform and to eliminate white streaks. (Be forewarned that the colors may stain wooden spoons.)

3   If you do make your icing too dark, add more plain, uncolored icing to the bowl to lighten. You can also add "super white" food coloring gel, but this will also lighten the tone of the color. This is important to note if you're matching flood and piping colors: If you've added "super white" to flood icing, you'll have to do the same to piping icing (and vice versa) to achieve the same tone.

4   When matching flood and piping icing colors, you'll need to add different amounts of food coloring to each to achieve the same color because of the two icings' different consistencies. Once again, add a drop at time until you arrive at your color match. Unfortunately, there are no precise formulas, which means you're going to have to eyeball the color every time.

PREPARING TO PIPE AND FLOOD

This section explains how to set up pastry bags and fill squeeze bottles. You'll need one pastry bag for each piping icing color and a squeeze bottle for each flood color. We like to set up our pastry bags ahead of time so that the minute our icing is colored, we're ready to fill them.

✻ FILLING A PLASTIC SQUEEZE BOTTLE
WITH FLOOD ICING

After you've colored your icing, simply pour the icing directly from the bowl into your squeeze bottle. If you don't have a steady pouring hand, use a funnel. Put the top on the squeeze bottle, and if it has a little cap to cover the squeeze hole, snap it on immediately as well. If the bottle doesn't have a cap, stick a toothpick in the squeeze-bottle hole to keep your icing from drying.

If you don't have squeeze bottles on hand, you can apply flood icing from the icing container with a spoon. This is a bit cumbersome and it requires a steady hand to avoid drips. Note that if you're using the spoon method, it's especially important to keep your icing colors covered when you're not using them.

✳ PUTTING THE TIP ON A PASTRY BAG

1 Unscrew the coupler and push the bigger threaded piece into the tip of the bag as far as it will go. (It should fit snugly; don't force it so far that you split the bag.)

2 Deeply score the bag with scissors just below the edge of the coupler. You now should be able to pull off the pastry bag tip about 2 inches from the end.

3 Place a metal pastry tip over the now-exposed opening of the threaded coupler piece and tightly screw the coupler ring over the tip and threads, catching the bag in the threads of the coupler in the process. If the coupler is on properly and tightly enough, the pastry tip should be stable (that is, it shouldn't wobble).

We highly recommend that you use couplers to simplify changing tips and cleanup and to keep the tip in place and secure. However, if you don't have a coupler, insert the tip into the pastry bag, and score the bag with your scissors approximately one-third of the way up from the pointy end of the tip. Don't go too far up, or the hole will be too big and the tip will fall out.

✳ FILLING THE PASTRY BAG WITH PIPING ICING

1 Hold the pastry bag, tip side down, in your nondominant hand. Cuff the bag over your fist.

2 Using a spoon, scoop the icing into the bag, making sure to stuff the icing as deep as you can toward the tip. We use a teaspoon because it's small and we can get it far down into the bag. You can use your thumb outside the bag to scrape what's on the spoon into the bag. Don't overfill the bag (a half-full bag is ideal), and try to avoid getting the icing toward the top of the bag. (It's not a tragedy if you do, but keeping the top of the bag clean tends to save some mess later.)

3 Unfold the bag and shake it firmly with a snapping motion so that the icing will move to the bottom of the bag. Then squeeze the bag closed at the top

Spooning icing into a pastry bag

of the icing mass and push the icing from the upper area of the bag toward the tip. (This will minimize any air pockets that could interrupt your icing flow.)

4　Twist the top of the bag closed and fasten it with a twist tie at the top of the icing. Tightly tie a second twist tie toward the top end of the bag to seal in any icing smears on the upper part of the bag. These smears will dry later, and without the second twist tie, they can flake dry colored icing onto wet cookies.

In a pinch, you can use a quart-sized zip-top freezer bag (not a thin sandwich bag) in place of a pastry bag. Insert the coupler and tip into one of the bottom corners of the bag, using the same method you use for a pastry bag. If you don't have a coupler and tip, cut the tiniest hole possible in the corner of the bag. This will allow you to pipe straight lines, outlines, dots, and other simple details.

Remember to press the air out of the bag and firmly seal the zip top before piping. Be aware that the shape of the bag sometimes generates odd air pockets, which can interrupt icing flow. A twist tie at the top of the icing mass in these makeshift bags will somewhat alleviate this problem.

✳ HOW TO HOLD AND SQUEEZE THE PASTRY BAG

If you've never used a pastry bag, it takes a little while to get accustomed to using it. The most effective way of holding the bag is to grab it with your dominant hand (right or left), so that your thumb wraps around the top of the icing. Hold the bag at a 45-degree angle to the cookie, and use the heel of your palm to apply pressure to squeeze out the icing and your other hand to steady and guide the tip. If you're making icing dots, hold the bag straight up and down (not at an angle).

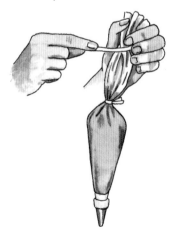

Closing the pastry bag with two twist ties

Holding and squeezing the pastry bag

decorating techniques

Like an artist who has just mixed her paints, now you're ready to create your cookie master-pieces. Grab your cookies, your icings, your other decorating add-ons, and your inspirational pictures as guides — or let your imagination run wild. If you've never used royal icing before, read our how-tos that follow. You can use our template to practice or go right to the cookies — remember that no matter what they look like, they'll still taste good!

Decorating Technique: PIPING

Piping is the technique we use most often, either to outline cookies to be flooded or to add embellishments to plain, undecorated cookies or to wet or dry flood icing. Basic piping takes practice. Here are some hints.

* Your pastry-bag tip shouldn't touch the cookie surface but rather should hover just above it as you pipe the icing onto the cookie.

* Different amounts of pressure make different line thicknesses. Refer to the chart on page 60 for information on which tips are best for specific piping tasks.

* For us, black coloring always seems to thin the icing a little more than other colors and also tends to bleed a little bit when it's piped onto wet icing. If you are piping precise black lettering, we advise that you use the smallest tip available — either a 00, 0, or 1 — and wait until the flood icing is completely dry before you begin.

* On the facing page you'll find a template of lines and shapes to give you piping practice.

piping practice template

Photocopy this page, lay the copy on a flat surface, and cover it with a piece of wax paper. Tape down the corners so the wax paper doesn't move. Pipe over the lines and loops to practice your piping technique.

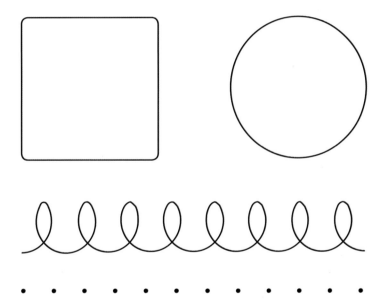

✳ **PIPING LEAVES.** For leaves, such as the holly leaves on the Christmas wreath, use a #67 leaf tip. Holding the flat side of the tip against the cookie, exert pressure to form the flat end of the leaf. Ease off the pressure as you pull the tip toward you. The leaf should thin to form the pointed end.

* **OUTLINING.** Outlining a cookie creates a dam to hold the flood icing. The goal is to pipe around the cookie shape in an unbroken line, trying to get the icing as close to the edge of the cookie as possible without it falling off. (If it does fall off, you can try to move it back on with a toothpick.) When the outline reaches the spot where you started, lift the bag to end your line. If you want a seamless line, use your toothpick to smooth out the connecting ends. You can also use piping to create decorative details on dry flood icing. Remember: Practice makes . . . better — and if you were perfect, nobody would like you much anyway.

* **PIPING HEARTS.** These are adorable and it takes just a minute to get the knack of making them. Simply pipe a short line for the left side of the heart, exerting a little more pressure at the start of the line and easing up at the end. Then make another line just like this for the right side of the heart, piping it to meet in a V with the first line.

* **PIPING BASKET WEAVE.** To create the base lines, pipe equidistant lines the length of your design. Using a wide, flat tip (such as a #45 or #46) to create the cross weave, pipe short lines over every other line, making sure to alternate lines with each row to create a woven effect.

* **PIPING ON WET PIPING.** We use this technique to create eyes on a cookie.

1 Pipe the following colors on top of one another in this order: white, an iris color (such as blue or brown), and black (for the pupil).

2 If you don't want "googly" eyes, wait a moment after piping the icing, then dip your finger in water and press on the eye very slightly to flatten it.

THE MIGHTY TOOTHPICK!

We find toothpicks indispensable for our cookie decorating. We use them to coax flood icing into narrow corners, to gently move errant outline icing to its proper place, to flatten little icing peaks that occur when you lift the tip away from a finished line, to neaten the edges of cookies before baking, and even to create designs on cookies. We always keep on hand containers of fresh toothpicks — round and flat — and we go through a bazillion (okay, at least a couple dozen) at each cookie craft session. Just make sure to use a fresh toothpick for each color of icing to prevent Jackson Pollock–esque cookies (unless, of course, that's your intention)!

Guiding icing with a toothpick

Cleaning cookie edges with a toothpick

Decorating Technique: FLOODING AND WORKING WITH FLOOD

Once your cookie is outlined, it's ready to be filled, if you choose.

1   Squeeze flood icing into the middle of the shape; it should flow toward the outline dam.

2   Use a small offset spatula or a toothpick to coax the icing into the corners and up to the edges of the shape. If you see any big air bubbles on the surface of the cookie, use the tip of a toothpick to puncture them.

Flooding a tree cookie

Filling all the corners

3   Remember to test first! If you're at all unsure of how to execute your design and don't want to mess up a good cookie, place a piece of wax paper over your cookie shape, trace it, and practice on the paper.

Drying. After being flooded, cookies have to dry undisturbed. Flood icing generally requires 2 to 3 hours of drying time before you can safely move cookies or add more layers of decorative detail without danger of smudging. Allow 24 hours for the icing to fully set before stacking, packing, or shipping the cookies. In humid weather, it may take even longer. You might be tempted to completely cover the cookies while you wait for them to fully set — DO NOT. This will slow the drying. If you're trying to keep away pet hair, see If You Have Pets on page 72.

✳ FLOODING ON WET FLOOD. Squeezing contrasting flood icing on wet flood creates a painterly effect that's effective for shapes such as hearts, Easter eggs, and ornaments. Try squeezing polka dots, stripes, or squiggles, or use a mighty toothpick to create the feathered effects described below. With flooding on wet flood, the colors will bleed into each other slightly — and may continue to bleed after drying. This is especially true of black (note the features of the Halloween skull on page 21), and you may want to take advantage of this effect in your cookie designs.

Creating Feathered Stripes on Wet Flood

1 Squeeze straight lines in a contrasting color on wet flood.

2 Draw a toothpick perpendicularly through the stripes.

Flooding straight lines on wet flood

Creating feathered effect with a toothpick

3 For a "houndstooth" effect, alternate toothpick direction with each row (as on Christmas ornaments #11 and #12; see pages 26–29).

Creating Feathered Dots (Hearts) on Wet Flood

1 Squeeze dots in a contrasting color on wet flood.

2 Draw a toothpick through the middle of each dot to create a heart shape. Create a string of hearts by lining up the dots and drawing the toothpick through them in one direction in a single motion.

Flooding dots

Feathering heart shapes

Creating Feathered Circles (Spiderwebs or Lace) on Wet Flood

1 Squeeze concentric circles in a contrasting color on wet flood.

2 Beginning at the center of the cookie, draw a toothpick through each line to the edge of the cookie to create a spiderweb effect. To create a lacy pattern, alternate the direction you use to draw the toothpick through each row.

Flooding circles

Feathering lace

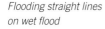

Combining Feathering Effects. You can combine techniques to create different effects. For instance, on holly leaves you can make short green lines, feather these outward, and add piped red dots as holly berries. (See cookie #8 on page 31.)

✳ **FLOODING OVER DRY PIPED DETAIL.** This effect reminds us of bead board and works well for cookies in house shapes.

1 Outline the cookie.

2 Pipe the design or detail on the cookie (for example, vertical lines for house siding).

3 When the piping is dry to the touch, flood the entire shape, letting the flood icing flow over the piped lines.

Piping house lines

Flooding over dry lines

✳ **ATTACHING ADD-ONS TO WET FLOOD.** Sugars and candy or nut add-ons stick readily to wet flood. Sprinkle sanding sugar on wet flood for a sparkly finish. To add dragees or confetti to wet flood, use tweezers to place items precisely. Tweezers are also helpful when you need to pick "mistakes" out of wet icing.

Attaching an ornament with tweezers

✳ **ATTACHING ADD-ONS TO DRY FLOOD.** After flood icing has dried, it's still possible to attach a variety of add-on details to cookies. Use a dab of royal icing to affix cookie add-ons, confetti, nuts, and candy. Make sure to allow the dab of icing to thoroughly dry after attaching the add-on.

Decorating Technique: USING FONDANT

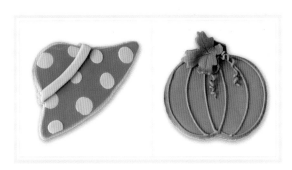

Fondant is a broadly used term referring to confections made from sugar syrup and used for decorating baked goods or filling candies. Here, we're referring to the popular, ready-made rolled fondant, which is widely available in a variety of colors. It is super easy to use — it's kind of like a child's edible play clay — and thus has the advantage of providing cookie crafters with instant creative gratification. We personally prefer to use it sparingly for small decorative details to allow the great taste of our cookies to shine through. Note that fondant dries out very quickly after it's opened; keep what you're not using in a sealed zip-top bag. Following are a variety of fondant decorating techniques to enable you to indulge your own preferences.

What you'll need to get started:

* ready-made rolled fondant in a variety of colors
* rolling pin and ⅛-inch cookie slats
* cookies and cutters in desired shapes
* pastry brush
* light corn syrup

✳ COVERING COOKIES WITH FONDANT

If you want to decorate a cookie entirely with fondant:

1 Roll out the fondant using the cookie slats.

2 Cut the fondant with the same cutter you used to cut the cookie so that the fondant shape matches the cookie shape.

3 With your pastry brush, lightly paint the cookie with corn syrup, then place the matching fondant on top and smooth it with your fingers. The corn syrup will "glue" the fondant in place.

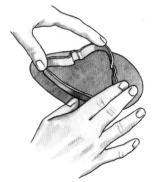

Cutting fondant in cookie shape

Attaching fondant to cookie

✻ CREATING DESIGNS WITH ROLLED FONDANT

It's easy to dress up your plain fondant with stripes or dots.

1   Roll out the dominant-color fondant as a base.

2   For dots and stripes, form desired shapes from contrasting colors. Roll small balls for dots; roll ropes for stripes.

3   Place the balls or ropes on the base fondant. Using the cookie slats on either side of the base fondant to ensure that you reach a uniform thickness, roll the balls or ropes into the base fondant to fuse the colors.

4   Cut as desired to cover the cookies.

Small fondant dots

Rolling out fondant dots

✻ CREATING CONTRASTING SHAPES WITH ROLLED FONDANT

To make distinct, detailed contrasting shapes:

1   Roll out your base-color fondant.

2   Using cookie cutters, cut desired shapes from the fondant.

3   Roll out contrasting-color fondant and cut out the same shapes you removed from the base.

4   Place the contrasting-color shapes into the shaped holes you cut in the base fondant, as you would jigsaw puzzle pieces. Then roll the base fondant and the contrasting fondant with your rolling pin and cookie slats to fuse the two.

✻ IMPRINTING FONDANT AND CREATING CUTOUTS

Use small cookie cutters, aspic cutters, or household objects to imprint designs in the fondant, in the same way that you imprint raw cookie dough (see page 88), or use them to make fondant cutouts that can be affixed onto cookies, such as flowers or a band on a hat.

✻ MAKING FONDANT DETAILS

Fondant can be sculpted into decorative details for cookies. You may have to practice a bit with shaping and sculpting these details, but in no time you can create fondant leaves and vines (such as those on the pumpkin on the previous page).

OTHER DECORATING TECHNIQUES

* **SUGARING AFTER BAKING.** To add sparkle to a plain cookie background, as on the champagne bottle, simply brush a little corn syrup on the cookie and sprinkle sugar on it. The syrup will be less sticky when it's dry.

* **USING FOOD-SAFE MARKING PENS.** These look just like magic markers and are especially good for decorating with small children and to quickly write a name on a cookie to personalize it. They write well both on plain cookies that haven't been iced and on dry flood icing.

* **PAINTING WITH LUSTER DUST OR PEARL DUST.** You can use luster or pearl dust on plain cookies or dry iced cookies.

To decorate cookies with luster or pearl dust:

1   Use a clean, dry paintbrush to scoop the dust into a small bowl.

2   Mix the dust with a few drops of clear spirits, such as vodka or clear extracts (these evaporate and dry quickly), until the dust is dissolved into a thin liquid.

3   Use the paintbrush to paint the luster dust onto a plain cookie or dry royal icing for a decorative metallic or pearlized effect. Alternatively, you can use a stencil to create a design.

Painting with luster dust

7

simple to showstopping
cookie craft constructions

With just a little bit more decorating or packaging effort, you can make your cookies into extra-special, giftable treats and favors. Surprise your dinner guests with edible place cards, send a message to a friend in tasty letters, or bestow delicious cookie pops on your favorite sports team. Or combine all the techniques you've learned in chapters 5 and 6 to create showstopping three-dimensional centerpieces or decorations that, just like old-fashioned gingerbread houses, are held together with royal icing.

All the ideas and instructions you'll find here are adaptable to cookie shapes for every occasion. When you're making favors or treats for a crowd, it's a good idea to make several extras in case of breakage. You can also use extra cookies as keepsakes for yourself or the guest of honor.

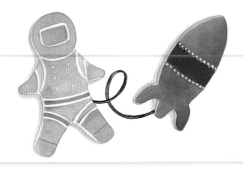

MULTICOOKIE CREATIONS

You can attach two or more cookies to each other to create detail and interest. To make these multi-cookie creations:

1 Bake and decorate each cookie separately (or decorate them before baking, if appropriate). For example, if you're attaching an astronaut to a spacecraft, pipe, flood, and decorate them separately. See the heart-on-heart Valentine's cookie (#4) on page 11 or the Halloween tombstone and jack-o'-lantern (#8) on page 21.

2 When all the cookies are cooled and dry, attach them to each other with royal icing. For example, for the astronaut and spacecraft, attach a licorice whip to the back of each cookie with a generous blob of royal icing. For the Valentine's heart or Halloween tombstone and jack-o'-lantern, use a blob of icing to "glue" the top cookie to the bottom one. Be sure to let the royal icing dry completely before moving cookies.

STAND-UP COOKIES AND
COOKIE PLACE CARDS

Special cookie cutters are available to make stand-up cookies, but we also make our own by using royal icing "glue" to affix an easelback to the cookie shapes we already own. See the cookie graveyard surrounding the Halloween haunted house luminaria on page 114. You can make any relatively flat-bottomed cookie shape — for example, the tiered cakes on page 36 or the teapots on page 17 — into a stand-up creation. See page 153 for easel templates; you can also create your own by cutting a rectangular or square cookie in half diagonally.

To make stand-up cookies:

1   Bake cookies in the desired shape. (Remember to make several more cookies than you need as backups in case a cookie breaks in the building process.) Bake an equal number of easelbacks; the height of these backs should be at least half that of the cookie.

2   Decorate the cookies as desired.

3   When the cookies are completely cooled, fully decorated, and dry, affix an easelback to each one with piping-consistency royal icing. Make sure to stand up the cookie for a second or two before the icing dries to ensure that you've placed the easelback for maximum steadiness, but dry the cookie face down (that is, easelback up). Once the icing "glue" is completely dry, the cookie will stand.

This method can be used to create edible place cards for special parties. Cut out rectangular cookies for simple, elegant designs or create a more whimsical place card. You can personalize place cards either before baking by cutting out or imprinting names or after baking using piped royal icing, luster dust, or food-safe markers to write the guests' names.

Easelback attached with icing

117

COOKIE MESSAGES

Sweet greetings are always welcome! Make and decorate cookie letters that spell out the desired message (such as *Happy Sweet 16, I ♥ You,* or *Joy*). Just be sure the message fits a shallow box for shipping (see the resources for suppliers).

1   Cut a piece of cardboard to fit the inside bottom of the box as closely as possible, and cover the cardboard with foil.

2   Dab royal icing on the back of the cookie letters (if they're iced, make sure they're completely dry), and affix the letters to the cardboard.

3   Let this icing "glue" dry completely, then wrap the message and foil backing in clear plastic wrap.

4   Place bubble cushioning on the bottom of the box. Place the foil-covered lettered cardboard on the bubble cushioning, then layer more cushioning on top. Seal the box and shake it gently. If the cardboard moves at all, add more padding. (If the cookies move, you're in trouble! Reglue them with royal icing and let the icing dry completely.) Seal the box, address it, and send it using your desired carrier (see chapter 8 for information on shipping carriers).

PARTY- OR SHOWER-FAVOR
COOKIE BOXES

These cookie boxes can hold small candies or other tiny items. Many shapes are tailor-made for party-favor boxes — for instance, baby carriages, pumpkins, or a child's alphabet blocks.

1 For each cookie box, you'll need three squares for the bottom, front, and back and two shapes for the sides. (Templates for boxes are on page 153). In the example shown here, the sides are baby carriages for shower favors. Make sure to bake the side shapes as mirror opposites.

2 When the cookies have cooled, decorate the sides, again as mirror opposites, and let them let dry completely.

3 In the meantime, using royal icing, glue together the box frames (a bottom, front, and back cookie for each). Let them dry completely (at least several hours); you can use your cookie slats or cans to support the frames while they dry, as shown.

4 Finally, glue two decorated sides to each frame, let the boxes dry overnight, then fill them with candy or any other treats.

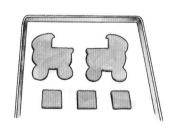

Baking the cookie shapes

Letting the cookie box frame dry

Gluing decorated cookies to the box frame

DOUBLE-SIDED COOKIE POPS

Each pop requires two cookies so that the pops will have two decorated sides. This means that you'll need to cut out twice the number of cookies as the desired number of finished pops. (For example, if you're making a dozen pops, you'll have to bake 24 cookies.) To make each pop:

1 Cut out two cookies of the same shape and place a lollipop stick under one of them, pressing down gently to embed the stick. (If you're making 12 pops, you'll attach sticks to 12 of your 24 cookies.)

2 Bake the cookies as directed.

3 After the cookies have cooled, decorate the top of each cookie as desired.

4 When they're completely dry, use royal icing to glue together the two cookies back to back — glue one with the stick to one without so that the stick is sandwiched between two cookies.

5 Let the royal icing dry thoroughly, then wrap the pops in cellophane.

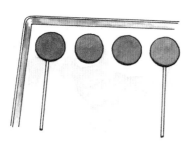

Sticks attached to half the cookies

Gluing cookies together

cookie craft showstoppers

Once you're comfortable with the techniques for decorating cookies, you can take your cookie crafting to the next level by creating multiple-stage cookies. We call these special cookie constructions our showstoppers.

A chocolate cookie bat hovers over our Halloween haunted house luminaria, which is made spookier with candy windowpanes and a witch flying across the moon on her broomstick. The Santa's sleigh centerpiece is made from tasty gingerbread and can be filled with numbered cookies for use as an Advent calendar or with festive wrapped candies or small packages.

We've included step-by-step instructions and templates to help you with your baking, decorating, and assembly. But don't stop the show there: Let these inspire you to create your own festive and impressive cookie craft constructions!

(For showstopper photo, see page 114)

Illuminated from behind with votive candles, this makes a great decoration for a Halloween side table or entryway. For the surrounding cookie graveyard, there are many possibilities — pumpkins, tombstones, ghosts, cats, and more. Allow at least two full days to complete this project; it will require several stages of drying. To make and assemble the haunted house, use the following checklist for supplies.

---

supplies checklist

- **1 recipe chocolate cookie dough** (page 79)

- **Templates:** haunted house (page 148), roof and house easel supports (page 149), cookie-graveyard easelbacks (page 153), and moon stencil for witch on a broomstick (page 152)

- **X-acto knife**

- **4 pastry bags** fitted with #2 tips

- **2 squeeze bottles**

- **Small spatula** or butter knife (for imprinting)

- **1 8-inch lollipop stick**

- **1 black food-safe marker** (optional — see instructions)

- **Yellow hard candies** (crushed for windowpanes; see page 89)

- **Bottle cap** (for imprinting)

- **Ingredients for ½-pound recipe royal icing, piping consistency** (page 97)

- **Ingredients for ½-pound recipe royal icing, flood consistency** (page 97)

- **Icing colors:** brown, orange, black, white

- **Small bat cookie cutter**

- **Witch silhouette cookie cutter**

- **Silver dragees**

- **Several heavy cans** (such as 28-ounce cans of tomatoes) for bracing

- **Assorted decorated cookies** for graveyard (ghosts, pumpkins, tombstones, cats, and so on)

- **2 small glass votive candleholders with candles**

1 Roll out the entire recipe of dough in one piece, ¼ inch thick, in a rough rectangle that's large enough for the house and roof stencils. Chill the dough until it's firm enough to cut (see Ready to Roll on page 83 for complete rolling and cutting instructions).

2 Preheat the oven to 350°F.

3 Using the house template and the X-acto knife, cut out the house. Cut out windows and the doorway, making sure to keep these shapes intact as you remove them with a knife or spatula and reserving them to use as shutters and the door when you assemble the house.

4 Using the roof template, cut out the roof of the house. Using the 3-inch round template, cut out the moon. Cut out the rectangular house support and the square door support, and cut each of these diagonally into two easel triangles. Cut out the bat and witch cookie.

5 Place the house on a parchment-lined cookie sheet so that the bottom is near one end. Gently slide 4 inches of the 8-inch lollipop stick under the dough on the top right side of house, so that 4 inches of the stick extends above the roof. Place the moon on top of the lollipop stick, leaving 2 inches of bare stick between the house and the moon. Gently press the house dough and moon dough to embed the stick in each, trying to minimize the lump caused by the stick while taking care not to crack the dough. (It's important that the moon be flat for flooding later on.)

Dough rolled out for house stencil

Cutting out the house, windows, and doorway

Removing windows and door

6 Fill the empty house windows with the crushed yellow hard candies. Using the bottle cap, imprint the roof to look like tiles. Using the spatula or knife, imprint the shutters and the door to represent slats and planks. Place all the remaining pieces — the witch, the bat, and anything else you're using in the yard — on a separate cookie sheet.

7 Bake all the pieces for 12–16 minutes or until the cookies start to turn a deeper brown around the edges. Make sure not to underbake the cookies; they must be firm when cooled (smaller cookies will be done more quickly). Leave all cookies on the cookie sheets to cool.

8 Make and divide the piping icing into two equal portions, and divide one of these again into three equal portions. Color the largest portion brown (this will be used for gluing the supports and other pieces to the house); color one smaller batch orange and another black, and leave one batch white. Fill pastry bags with the colored piping icings.

9 Make the flood icing. Color about ⅓ cup of the flood icing black and leave ⅓ cup white. Fill the squeeze bottles with the colored flood icing. **NOTE:** You'll make more flood icing than you'll need. Color only what the house requires and use the remainder for other cookies.

10 When they are fully cooled, ice the cookies right on the baking sheet. Pipe and flood the moon with white icing. Affix the shutters with brown royal icing. Affix the door easel to the door with brown royal icing, and allow it to dry with the door facing down and the support standing up in the air. Pipe and flood the bat; add silver dragee eyes. Let these dry completely.

11 When the moon is dry, affix the witch cookie to it with royal icing. Affix the roof with brown royal icing, butting the top edge of the roof against the moon. Use plenty of icing to "caulk" the bottom of the roof to the top of the house. The roof will be slightly pitched.

12 Let the entire assembly dry completely, preferably overnight.

13 When the house is completely dry, carefully flip it over so it's face down and apply additional icing to the lollipop stick, the roof, and the back of the moon to reinforce these elements. Attach the side supports to the house with brown icing, making sure the bottoms of the supports are flush with the bottom of the house so that the

Drying the haunted house

simple to showstopping cookie craft constructions

luminaria won't wobble when it's standing. Brace the supports with heavy cans on the sides to ensure that they dry in a stable position. Let the assembly dry completely — the piping icing must be rock hard.

Drying the supports

14 When the house is dry, stand the luminaria on a flat surface. Pipe around the roof tiles with black and orange icing to outline them. Pipe around the windows with orange icing, if desired. Glue the bat to the roof and the dragee hinges onto the door with brown piping icing. Stand the door in front of the house doorway (its easel will support it). Stand the graveyard cookies, bats, ghosts, and pumpkins at either side of the house.

15 Place the votive candles in the candleholders behind the house. Light them, and be very afraid!

SANTA'S SLEIGH CENTERPIECE

Who doesn't like to get gifts from Santa? Our Santa's sleigh centerpiece is designed to hold holiday treats — wrapped candies or decorated cookies. You can make the centerpiece an Advent calendar with any small cookies you wish, from snowflakes to candy canes and stockings. Each day in December a lucky someone gets to pick and eat the day's cookie. Just number the cookies 1 through 24, and don't forget to make a star for the number 24. Small round cookies can be decorated as ornaments, and small squares can be packages for Santa to deliver. You can even fill the sleigh with black licorice candies to resemble coal!

Allow two days to complete this project. To make and assemble Santa's sleigh and the cookies in it, use the following checklist for supplies.

supplies checklist

- **1 recipe gingerbread cookie dough,** divided into two portions (see page 82 for recipe; this is enough to make the sleigh and 24 one-inch miniature cookies)

- **Templates** for Santa's sleigh centerpiece (pages 150–151)

- **X-acto knife**

- **2 pastry bags fitted with #2 tips**

- **2 squeeze bottles**

- **Clean paintbrush**

- **Ingredients for ½-pound recipe royal icing, piping consistency** (page 97)

- **Ingredients for ½-pound recipe royal icing, flood consistency** (page 97)

- **Christmas red food coloring**

- **White sanding sugar**

- **Silver luster dust**

- **2 tuna cans and several heavy cans** (such as 28-ounce cans of tomatoes) for bracing

- **½ ounce clear spirits** (such as vodka or clear extract)

- **Wrapped candies or small decorated cookies** (to fill sleigh), numbered 1–24 (optional, for Advent calendar)

- **24 candy-sized cellophane bags and ties** (to wrap cookies)

1 Roll each of the two gingerbread portions into a ¼-inch-thick rectangle that's large enough for the template of the sleigh side. Chill until the dough is firm enough to cut (see Ready to Roll on page 83 for complete rolling and cutting instructions).

2 Preheat the oven to 350°F.

3 Using the template and an X-acto knife, cut out one sleigh side from the first piece of dough, and place it on a parchment-lined cookie sheet. Flip the template and cut out a mirror image of the first sleigh side from the other piece of dough; place it on another parchment-lined cookie sheet. Cutting mirror images ensures that you'll be icing the top of each cookie in the correct orientation for the finished sleigh. Gather the

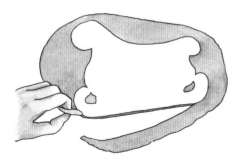

Cutting out one sleigh side

remaining dough, roll it, and use the templates to cut out the sleigh box pieces (five in all); place them on a third parchment-lined cookie sheet. Use any remaining dough to roll and cut the 24 miniature cookie shapes to fill the sleigh, if desired.

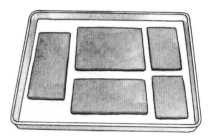

The five pieces of the sleigh box

4 Bake the pieces for 12–16 minutes or until the cookies start to turn a deeper brown around the edges. Do not underbake them; the cookies must be firm when cool (small cookies will be done more quickly). Cool the sleigh pieces completely before icing. We recommend that you cool the pieces on the cookie sheets in order to avoid warping the warm cookies when you move them.

5 Make and divide the piping icing into two portions; color one portion red, and leave the other portion white. Fill pastry bags with the colored piping icings.

6 Make and divide the flood icing into two portions; color one portion red, and leave the other portion white. Fill squeeze bottles with the colored flood icings.

BAKING COOKIES
FOR CONSTRUCTION

When baking for a gingerbread construction project (like the Santa's sleigh center-piece), we like a harder cookie. We recommend that you omit the baking soda and bake the gingerbread closer to 16 minutes than to 12 (depending on your oven) to ensure that you get consistently crisp cookies. Just keep an eye on the cookies as they bake to make sure they don't burn.

7 Using the red icings, pipe and flood the middle portion of each sleigh side and the front and rear box pieces.

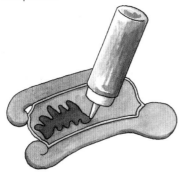

Flooding the center of the sleigh with red icing

8 Once the red icing has set for an hour or more, pipe and flood the top trim on each sleigh side with white icing, and sprinkle it with white sanding sugar while it is wet, being careful not to get sanding sugar on the red flood. While the white icing is setting, paint each sleigh runner with luster dust (see page 113 for instructions on using luster dust). Let all the icing dry completely.

Flooding the top of the sleigh

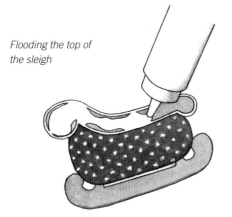

9 When the icing is dry, pipe white dots on the red sleigh sides and the front and rear box pieces. Sprinkle the dots with sanding sugar while they are wet. Pipe white outline details on the trim of each sleigh side. When the icing is dry, brush off any excess sanding sugar.

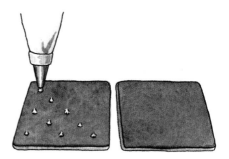

Piping white dots . . .

and sprinkling with sanding sugar

10 With white piping icing, affix the two long sides of the box to the box bottom. **NOTE:** The bottom edges of the side pieces should rest on the top of the bottom piece, rather than being glued alongside the bottom. (See the illustration accompanying the templates on page 151.) Next, affix the red decorated front and back pieces to the box. Brace the box with heavy cans while it dries overnight.

11 The next day, place the sleigh box on two tuna cans to prop it to the correct position against the sleigh sides. Using white piping icing, attach the decorated sides of the sleigh to the box. Brace this assembly with heavy cans while it dries overnight.

12 If you've made Advent cookies, decorate them as desired (including piped numbers, 1–24), and allow them to dry completely.

13 Wrap each mini Advent cookie or other cookies in cellophane and tie it decoratively. Place the wrapped cookies or any candies you choose inside the finished sleigh.

Drying the sleigh box

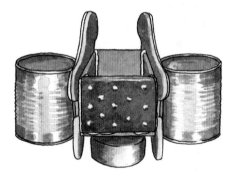

Drying the finished sleigh

8

freezing, storing, wrapping, and shipping

At cookie-decorating crunch time — holidays or special occasions or any time for a busy mom — baking ahead and freezing ensures that your cookies will be ready when the time is right for you to decorate. If your friends and family are lucky enough to be getting a cookie gift from you, here's how to wrap, store, and safely ship your fragile cookie creations.

FREEZING BAKED COOKIES

We prefer to freeze our cookies after baking them; because our roll-chill-cut method (chapter 4) is so quick and convenient, we find it easiest to mix the dough and bake the cookies all at once. This also ensures that our cookies will be ready for decorating when our schedules allow. It's great to have an undecorated batch of round cookies in the freezer for impromptu special occasions.

To freeze baked cookies, layer them in a flat, sturdy, covered container with wax paper between the layers. We use 9- by 13-inch covered cake pans for this; the lids are sturdy enough to stack without fear of crushing fragile cookies. We do not recommend freezing decorating cookies.

FREEZING UNBAKED COOKIE DOUGH

As noted in the chart Make-Ahead Tips on page 69, unbaked cookie dough can be frozen for up to two months. Be sure to wrap the flattened disks of dough tightly in plastic and then wrap them again in aluminum foil for protection from freezer burn. Label each package with the type of dough and the date and place it in a zip-top plastic bag. For best results, before working the dough, thaw the wrapped and packaged disks in the refrigerator overnight, then let them stand at room temperature until they're pliable enough to roll. Wipe off any condensation that may have formed on the outside of the package before you unwrap it to prevent moisture from dripping on dough.

You can also freeze unbaked cut-out cookies in a single layer on a wax-paper-lined cookie sheet. After they're frozen, layer the shapes in a flat, sturdy, covered container with wax paper between the layers. Note that the shapes will be brittle and fragile when frozen. (In addition, if your freezer is always jam-packed like ours are, there will be the constant danger that the cookies will tip or fall out when you open the door!) Because the cookies will thaw quickly once they're removed from the freezer, you don't have to defrost them before baking. They might take an extra minute or two in the oven, but check for doneness at the earliest time just in case.

STORING AND WRAPPING DECORATED COOKIES

Before storing or wrapping decorated cookies, make sure any royal icing decoration is completely dry — any residual moisture will prevent icing from completely hardening when packaged.

✳ STORING DECORATED COOKIES

Store decorated cookies in airtight containers at room temperature. If you're not going to eat or deliver or ship them within a week or so, we recommend freezing undecorated cookies and decorating them just before you need them. We've found that after two weeks, decorated cookies lose their freshness, although they're safe to eat for much longer. A little staleness has never stopped us from eating

COOKIE FAVORS

Clear cellophane bags are available in a variety of sizes and make an attractive presentation for your works of cookie art. Tie the bags with festive ribbons or even a bit of tulle to create fun — and edible — party or shower favors. Personalized ribbons are available from a variety of retailers (see the resources) — don't forget to order these ahead of time! Cellophane bags are also perfect to use as individual cookie packaging for safe shipping.

a cookie, but when we're serving them to others or giving them as gifts, we want them to be as fresh as possible.

❋ WRAPPING DECORATED COOKIES

If you're arranging your cookies on a plate for presentation, we recommend wrapping them completely in clear plastic (rather than foil or wax paper) to minimize exposure to air. The plastic also allows your handiwork to show through! Again, make sure cookies are completely dry before wrapping them.

SHIPPING DECORATED COOKIES

We've never met anyone who doesn't like getting a box of delicious decorated cookies in the mail, whether for a special occasion or just for fun. Here's what we've learned about sending our cookies out into the world.

IN COOKIES AS IN LIFE,
SOMETIMES THE COOKIE CRUMBLES

Let's face it: Breakage happens. We combat this inevitability by making and decorating a few extra cookies, especially when we need a certain number (for party favors, for example). Even if a cookie or two crumbles during shipping, however, remember that broken cookies still taste good!

❋ CHOOSING SHAPES

Decorated sugar cookies are fragile — especially cookies with thin shapes or appendages (for example, the tail and legs on a dog or the stem of a champagne glass). If you're planning to ship your cookies, we suggest you choose sturdy shapes with a minimum of thin appendages to reduce the danger of your cookies breaking en route.

❋ PACKING IN TINS

Tins serve two main purposes: They help keep cookies fresh and they help protect them from breaking in transit. There are a variety of attractive tins available in all shapes and sizes. While round tins are most common, we prefer rectangular tins, which allow cookies to fit better and which fit more easily in shipping boxes. See the resources for places where you can buy cookie tins.

Boxing and Adding Padding. We save clean bubble wrap, polystyrene or cornstarch peanuts, perforated "honeycomb" packing paper, newspapers, and sturdy boxes. Reusing these materials is kinder on our environment and saves considerable money on cookie packing. If you don't have boxes and packing materials on hand, they're readily available at many office supply stores and shipping centers.

Here are just a few of the cookies you can create with a flat-bottomed oval cookie cutter. If you can't find a cutter that's this shape, use the template on page 152.

✳ PREPPING PACKAGES FOR SHIPPING

We have two words for you: double padding. To minimize cookie breakage, we make sure there's plenty of packing material both inside the cookie tin and between the tin and the shipping box. Make sure to choose a box that allows a couple of inches of air on all sides of your cookie tin. Cookie-tin retailers sell boxes designed to snugly fit specific cookie tins — but DO NOT use these! Our tests resulted in broken cookies.

The how-to for optimal tin packing.

1. This step is optional but makes an attractive package. Cut a strip of wrapping paper to fit the inside width of the box and long enough to wrap around the box. Place the wrapping paper inside the cookie tin, face down, with the flaps outside the box.

2. Place a layer of crumpled wax paper on the bottom of the tin. It doesn't have to be a deep layer.

3. Place another sheet of wax paper in the tin, as if you were putting tissue paper in a gift box, but instead of making it neat, crumple it to fit against the sides of the tin.

4. Add your first layer of cookies. If you haven't put your cookies in individual cellophane bags (see Cookie Favors on page 135), wrap each one in a small piece of wax paper to prevent it from jostling against other cookies in the tin. Add small, crumpled pieces of wax paper to any pockets of space to prevent cookie movement.

5. Place another crumpled piece of paper on top of the packaged cookies, and then add another layer of cookies. Repeat until the box is nearly full. Make sure the cookies lie flat and apart from each other and leave at least ¾ inch between the top layer of cookies and the top of the tin to allow for more protective padding (such as bubble cushioning, "honeycomb" paper, or more crumpled wax paper). Add this layer of padding, then fold over the flaps of wrapping paper to cover the padding.

6. Cover with the lid and gently shake the tin. If you feel no movement, shake it a little harder. If you feel movement, open the tin, add more padding under the wrapping paper, and do the "shake" test again until you feel no movement inside the tin. If you feel no movement, open the tin, tape down the wrapping paper, and you're ready to pack the tin in the shipping box

7. IMPORTANT: Attach your gift note to the top of the tin *now,* before you pack your tin in the shipping box. All too often we've reopened and unpacked cookie boxes to add the note!

freezing, storing, wrapping, and shipping

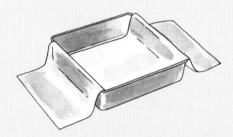

A layer of wrapping paper makes a pretty package

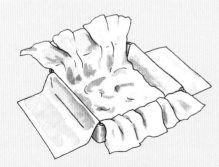

Crumpled wax paper cushions the cookies

The how-to for optimal box packing.

1 Choose a box that allows at least 2 to 3 inches of space around the tin on all sides and at the top and bottom.

2 Pad the bottom of the box with a healthy layer of packing peanuts, packing paper, or bubble cushioning.

3 Place the cookie tin in the box (with the gift note attached!), and thoroughly pad the space between the tin and the sides of the box.

4 Pad the top tightly and seal the box. Shake the package gently. If you feel no movement, shake it a little harder. If you feel movement, open the box and add more padding where needed, then close and seal the box, slap on the address label, and send it off with your fingers crossed!

freezing, storing, wrapping, and shipping

Here are just some of the cookies you can create with a round cookie cutter.

✳ SHIPPING THE PACKAGE

We love our postal workers and our UPS and Federal Express delivery people. After all, who doesn't like getting packages, and who doesn't appreciate prompt, careful delivery? Any of these delivery people will get your cookies to their destination, and all offer a variety of pricing and time options. Note that any guaranteed service requires extra time during the holidays, so plan for it.

United States Postal Service. The United States Postal Service (USPS) offers a number of shipping advantages, among them relatively low cost and convenience. We've found Priority Mail to be reliable and a great cookie-shipping value — especially because the boxes are free.

Priority Mail box #7 is a good size for many standard cookie tins. The Priority Mail flat-rate rectangular box (11 by 8½ inches by 8½ inches) is perfect for rectangular tin #4 (available from cookietins.com; see the resources). The cost to ship this flat-rate box remains the same no matter what the weight of the contents. Note, however, that because flat-rate Priority Mail costs the same whether the package is delivered locally or across the country, shipping cookies short distances might be less expensive with a non-flat-rate option. We suggest you compare delivery costs for both flat and nonflat rates.

Priority Mail shipping also offers a tracking option, which we always take advantage of. Note that in some areas, the USPS also offers free package pickup and free delivery of packing supplies. Be forewarned: The supplies can take several weeks to arrive, so plan ahead or simply go to your post office to pick up shipping supplies.

United Parcel Service. We love seeing the brown United Parcel Service (UPS) truck at our doors! The costs of UPS delivery services vary depending on package weight, destination, and delivery time. UPS offers several guaranteed-delivery services that are not inexpensive, but if you want your cookies delivered by a certain date, UPS is worth considering. Check your local listing for nearby UPS Stores or UPS service centers.

Federal Express. Federal Express (FedEx) offers ground shipping options in addition to overnight delivery services, and these are priced competitively with UPS. Next Day delivery is an expensive choice for cookie shipping, but when you need it there tomorrow, FedEx comes through.

9

cookie craft events

You can host a group cookie-decorating session for a special reason —
a fun birthday celebration, a cookie swap, or in preparation for a cookie
sale, for instance, or simply to get people together for some creative enjoyment. Cookie crafting can also be the means for raising funds for a good
cause. As for all get-togethers, planning ahead means less stress during
the festivities, so take a look at our hints and suggestions on how to throw
a successful cookie craft event.

COOKIE CRAFT PARTIES

Because your guests will be decorating and probably standing for much of the party, make any party food you offer easy on both yourself and them. Keep the menu casual and make-ahead and/or takeout so it can be served and eaten with a minimum of fuss, utensils, and cleanup.

✳ **GETTING READY FOR A PARTY.** If you plan ahead, you can have most of the materials and items ready the day before. Refer to the lists of ingredients and pantry supplies and equipment in chapter 2 for all required baking and decorating items. Here's an outline for what to prepare for maximum efficiency and fun at the party.

party prep timeline

UP TO THREE MONTHS BEFORE

❭ Bake the cookies. (These can be done far ahead of time and frozen; see page 134.)

THE NIGHT BEFORE

❭ Prepare pastry bags (one for each piping color).

❭ Set out plastic squeeze bottles (one for each flood color).

❭ Set up the table. Designate a spot on the perimeter for each person decorating, and lay out sturdy paper plates to use as convenient decorating surfaces. (The paper plates are also handy to use for transporting cookies to the drying area.)

❭ Set up a party food and eating area that's separate from your decorating area. This prevents food crumbs and spills near decorated cookies and decorating supplies.

TWO HOURS BEFORE

❭ Fill clear plastic cups with sprinkles, jimmies, dragees, and other add-ons. If you don't have bottles with shaker tops for your colored sugars, you can fill plastic cups with these and add a plastic spoon to each for application.

❭ Make piping royal icing; cover and refrigerate.*

❭ Make flood royal icing; cover and refrigerate.*

* If you're really pressed for time, you can make these the night before, but see our caveats on page 100.

ONE HOUR BEFORE

You might want to have a couple of sets of extra hands for this preparation.

❭ Color icings.

❭ Fill pastry bags with piping colors.

❭ Fill squeeze bottles with flood colors.

❭ Set out the refreshments.

✳ IT'S PARTY TIME. Some people were born with a pastry bag in their hands; others will need decorating guidance, especially if they've never used royal icing. It's a good idea to start with a few simple lessons for those who've never decorated before.

* A brief tutorial on outline piping and flooding plus a couple of other royal icing techniques is useful for almost everyone.

* Steer those less skillful decorators to the sugar add-ons and food-safe markers — even if they're not adept with the pastry bag, they can still have plenty of fun.

* We find it's best to start off with decorating for an hour or so, then steer the guests toward the refreshments. This allows cookies some time to dry so that guests can take home a few of their creations. Our guests tend to wander back to the decorating area after they've had something to eat.

* To make your decorating fun last past the party time, take photos of your guests in action as well as pictures of the finished cookies. Digital cameras and Internet photo-sharing services make it easy to circulate the party photos. You can also use the photos to create cookie photo cards or invitations to future cookie craft events. You can even create customized cookie-crafted stamps for the postage! Many photo services will also put your cookie images on coasters, playing cards, mugs, or mousepads. Use these for seasonal gifts or cookie craft party favors. See the resources for a selection of these services.

> ## COOKIE CRAFT PARTIES
> # FOR KIDS

Celebrate a birthday, or host a session to make 100 cookies for the 100th Day of School. Kids' cookie craft parties flow much the same as those for adults — and surprisingly, kids' attention spans don't vary too much from those of their adult decorating counterparts!

* Estimate that after an hour all but the most dedicated crafty kids will lose interest in decorating. Have the refreshments ready!

* While no doubt you'll be familiar with your guests' food allergies, overall we suggest you bake nut-free cookies for kids' gatherings to avoid any potential nut-allergy situations.

* Have plenty of sanitary wipes on hand, and keep reminding the kids to use them, both for the sake of the furniture and for everyone's health!

* Award prizes to each child. We've made them up as we go along, based on the cookie creations at each gathering. For example, you might give awards for Most Creative Use of Piping Icing or Best Use of Seasonal Colors. Just make sure nobody's feelings get hurt — no booby prizes!

* Have goody bags for all to take home — and include cookie cutters, of course!

* Make sure to take plenty of pictures and share them with the children both at the party (easy if you have a photo printer) and afterward.

COOKIE SWAPS

The basic idea of a cookie swap is that each guest brings a designated quantity of one type of cookie. The cookies are pooled, and each guest leaves with the same quantity he or she came with, this time a representative sampling of the cookies everyone has brought. Cookie swaps are great around the holidays; you'll wind up with a variety of cookies in the house, but you'll have to bake and decorate only one kind.

❋ GETTING READY FOR A SWAP

❋ What better way to invite people to a cookie swap than to put a photo of your own cookies on the invitation?

❋ Establish how many cookies each person should bring. Three dozen? Five dozen? Include this information on the invitation, and ask everyone to let you know what kind (or shape) of cookie they are decorating for the swap. (It's nice to avoid duplicates, though remember that the same cookies can look vastly different depending on each person's unique decorating flair.)

❋ Remind guests to bring copies of the recipes and a brief description of how the cookie is decorated, and let them know how many copies they should bring (based on the number of guests).

❋ Provide containers for each person to use to bring home his or her cookie loot, or tell people to bring an extra container of their own. Pretty tins or boxes can serve as party favors. Inexpensive aluminum containers and baggies can also work as take-home packaging.

❋ Provide snacks and drinks so people won't be tempted to eat *all* the cookies they're supposed to be taking home (though of course, a few will disappear)!

❋ IT'S PARTY TIME

❋ Arrange all the cookies on a table, with copies of the recipe near each one.

❋ If you're providing take-home containers or baggies, hand them out before the swap and let everyone know how many cookies to take of each variety on the table. To figure this out, divide the number of cookies each person has brought by the number of people attending the party. For example, if everyone brings three dozen cookies (36) and 15 people attend, each person takes home 2 of each variety of cookie (36 divided by 15 equals 2.4).

❋ If you have leftover cookies (those .4's!) your guests can either eat these along with the party treats you provide or take home an extra of their favorite cookie.

IN COOKIES AS IN LIFE,
REMEMBER *THE* [COOKIE] *DESIDERATA*

*If you compare your cookies to others,
you may become vain and bitter,
for always there will be greater and
lesser cookies than your own.
(Apologies to Max Ehrmann.)*

BAKE SALES

Because some commercially decorated cookies command a high retail price, selling decorated cookies at a bake sale can be a great way to raise money for a school activity or church or other organization. Here are some of our favorite suggestions and hints.

* Bake and decorate shapes that can be personalized on-site. For example, bake and ice Christmas stockings (at least a day ahead of time) and leave room to write names of cookie purchasers or cookie recipients on the cuff of each stocking. Because food-safe markers dry instantly, they're great for this purpose.

* In addition to selling finished cookies, you can outline and flood seasonal shapes ahead of time (pumpkins or Christmas tree ornaments, for example) and allow children at the sale to decorate their own cookies. Again, food-safe markers are great because there's no waiting time for drying.

* Select your shapes to coordinate with specific school fund-raising events. For instance, if a bake sale will benefit a sports team or raise money for gym equipment, footballs, soccer balls, baseballs, and basketballs would be fun choices. Cookie cutters are also available in music notes and instrument shapes for band fund-raisers — you get the idea.

* Set prices according to what your customer base will bear. Your bake sale might support 2 or 3 dollars per cookie, depending on how elaborately it's decorated — or you may be able to price your cookies much higher. It's for a good cause, after all!

* Presentation is important. Wrap finished cookies ahead of time in individual cellophane bags tied with ribbon. If you're personalizing cookies, have bags and ribbon on hand for wrapping once the name is written on them.

* You may want to create a showstopper as a centerpiece and raffle item. Give a ticket to anyone who buys a cookie.

* When transporting cookies, remember that they're fragile. Make sure to pack and move them carefully or your charitable efforts will be for naught!

TEMPLATES

Both Halloween templates exactly fit on an 8½" × 11" piece of paper.

HALLOWEEN HAUNTED HOUSE LUMINARIA
house front

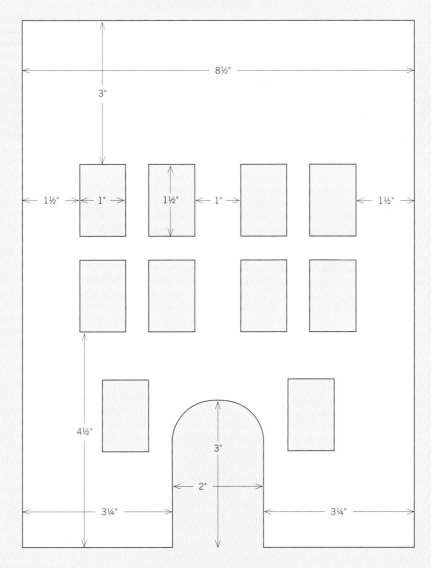

make photocopy at 200% of size shown

TEMPLATES

HALLOWEEN HAUNTED HOUSE LUMINARIA
roof and house supports

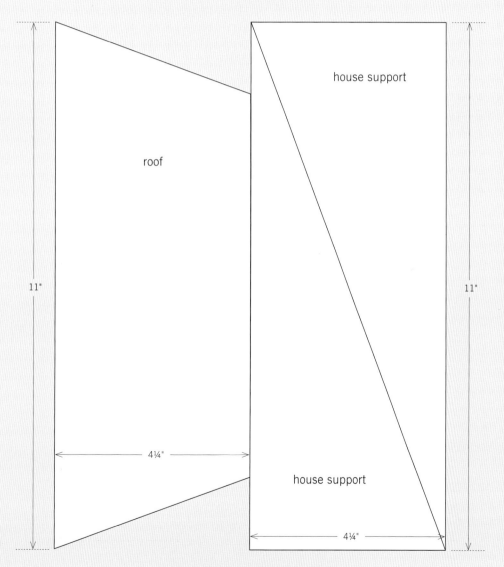

roof

house support

house support

11"

11"

4¼"

4¼"

make photocopy at 200% of size shown

TEMPLATES

SANTA'S SLEIGH CENTERPIECE
sleigh side

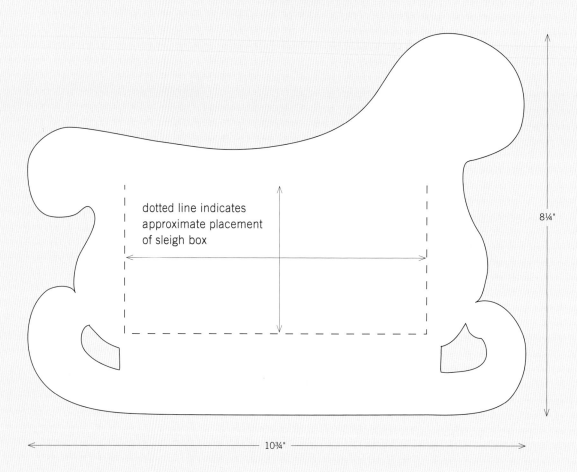

dotted line indicates
approximate placement
of sleigh box

8¼"

10¾"

make photocopy at 200% of size shown

TEMPLATES

SANTA'S SLEIGH CENTERPIECE
sleigh front, back, sides, and bottom

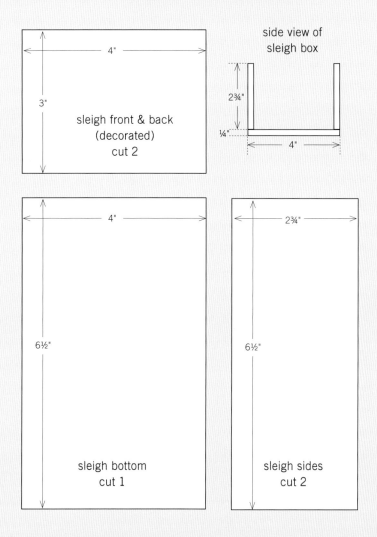

side view of
sleigh box

4"

3"

sleigh front & back
(decorated)
cut 2

2¾"

¼"

4"

4"

6½"

sleigh bottom
cut 1

2¾"

6½"

sleigh sides
cut 2

make photocopy at 200% of size shown

TEMPLATES

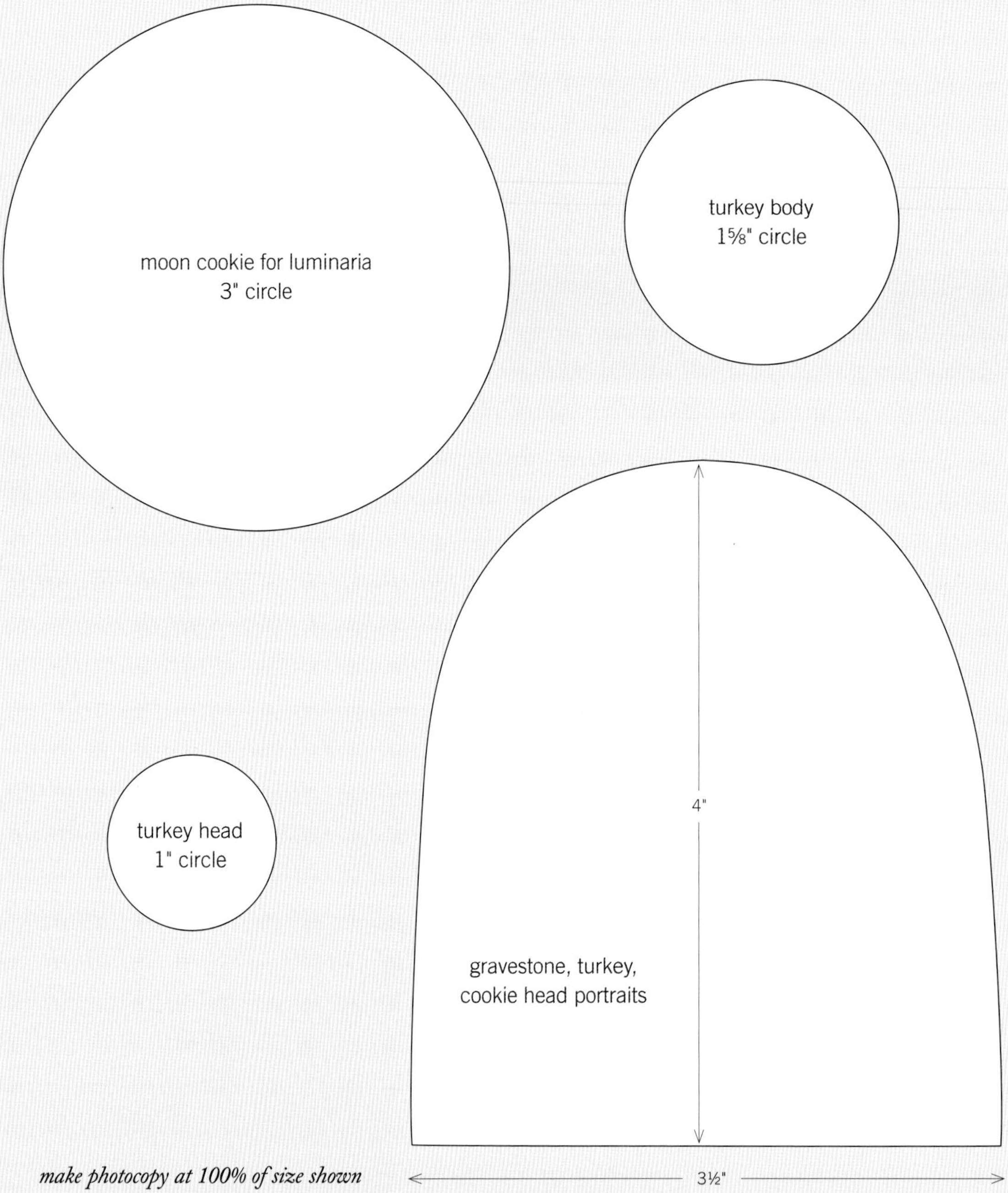

moon cookie for luminaria
3" circle

turkey body
1⅝" circle

turkey head
1" circle

4"

gravestone, turkey,
cookie head portraits

3½"

make photocopy at 100% of size shown

TEMPLATES

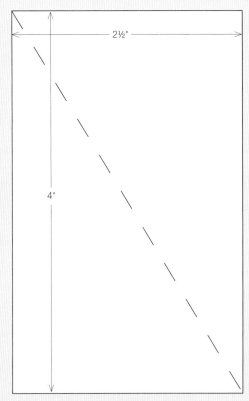

2½"

4"

place card or large easelback
(cut on line to make easelback)

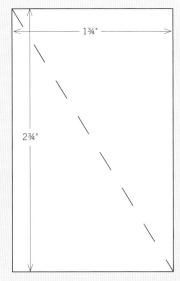

1¾"

2¾"

place card or medium easelback
(cut on line to make easelback)

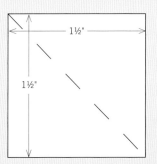

1½"

1½"

party-favor box side or small easelback
(cut on line to make easelback)

make photocopy at 100% of size shown

resources

This is by no means a comprehensive list, but these are stores and Web sites that have good selections.

A. C. Moore, Hobby Lobby, JoAnn's Fabrics & Crafts, Michael's

These and other craft stores (found in many locations) are now carrying a wide range of baking and decorating supplies — including ⅛-inch wooden slats that can be used for rolling out fondant. Browse the other craft aisles for inspiration or for items such as stencils that you can use for cookie decorating.

Ateco

www.atecousa.com
Ateco offers a comprehensive line of cookie cutters, pastry bags, tips, and other baking and decorating products.

Broadway Panhandler

866-266-5927
www.broadwaypanhandler.com
A New York institution for cookware and baking supplies.

Chef Central

914-328-1376
www.chefcentral.com
We wish there were more of these stores. They have a huge selection and good prices.

Chefs Catalog

800-338-3232
www.chefscatalog.com
A good online sourse for cookware and baking suppies.

The Container Store

888-266-8246
www.containerstore.com
Both the online shop and the bricks-and-mortar Container Store carry a wide variety of wrapping and packing materials, including tins, shipping boxes, and bubble cushioning.

The Cookie Cutter Shop

360-652-3295
www.cookiecuttershop.com
This site offers a large selection of metal cutters.

A Cook's Companion

197 Atlantic Avenue
Brooklyn, NY 11201
718-852-6901
This lovely and amazingly well-stocked store is in Janice's neighborhood in Brooklyn, and owner Jen has patiently answered zillions of Janice's questions and gone out of her way to order special equipment for us.

Cookietins.com

832-518-2800
www.cookietins.com
A great source for tins of all sizes and other cookie-packing accessories.

Cooking.com

800-663-8810
www.cooking.com
This site has a broad selection of cookware and bakeware; it also carries mesh food tents.

CopperGifts.com

620-421-0654
www.coppergifts.com
A great site for copper cutters in a variety of sizes and other cookie supplies. The company will also make custom cookie cutters for you.

The Great American Spice Company

877-677-4239
www.americanspice.com
This is a great source of 1-pound bags of sanding sugar in a variety of colors at great prices. If you don't need large quantities and you want to save even more money, buy the white sanding sugar and color your own.

Hardware stores

We get our cookie slats here.

H. O. Foose Tinsmithing Co.

610-944-1960
www.foosecookiecutters.com
We love the inexpensive metal cutters, and they have a huge selection. They also sell a kit to enable you to make your own custom cookie-cutter shapes.

Improvements

800-634-9484
www.improvementscatalog.com
A catalog for problem-solving household items; this was Janice's source for mesh food tents.

King Arthur Flour Company
800-827-6836
www.kingarthurflour.com
The King Arthur Flour site is a good source for two of our favorite items: parchment sheets that exactly fit a half-sheet pan and a foldable cooling rack.

Kitchen Collectables
888-593-2436
http://kitchengifts.com
A source of copper cookie cutters and other cookie-making supplies.

Kitchen Krafts
800-776-0575
www.kitchenkrafts.com

Kmart, Target, Wal-mart
These stores can be found in many locations. We like storing our cookies in the 9-inch × 13-inch covered cake pans available in their bakeware sections.

Kodak EasyShare Gallery
www.kodakgallery.com
For your cookie photo needs.

Name Maker
800-241-2890
www.namemaker.com
This is one of the many sites from which personalized ribbons are available. An Internet search will turn up other choices.

Off the Beaten Path
866-756-6543
www.cookiecutter.com
This site has a wide selection of metal cutters at reasonable prices.

ShoppersChoice.com
877-743-2269
www.shopperschoice.com
A general shopping Web site, and a source for mesh food tents.

Shutterfly
888-225-7159
www.shutterfly.com
A source for prints of your cookies pictures, party invitations, mugs, and so forth.

Sugarcraft
www.sugarcraft.com
Over 25,000 products including hard-to-find baking tools, ingridients, and supplies.

Supermarkets
All supermarkets carry the staples for cookie baking and decorating: flour, butter, sugar, confectioners' sugar, cocoa powder, extracts, and so forth. While meringue powder is not usually found at the supermarket, pasteurized egg whites and powdered egg whites are widely available.

Sur La Table
800-243-0852
various locations and online at
www.surlatable.com
Both the online shop and bricks-and-mortar cookware stores are well stocked with pans, cutters, decorating tips and bags, and other cookie necessities. We found the sometimes hard-to-find silver dragees here.

United States Postal Service
800-275-8777
www.usps.com
You can track USPS Priority Mail packages, schedule a package pickup, order mailing supplies (many free of charge), and even print address labels directly from the site.

Williams-Sonoma
877-812-6235
www.williams-sonoma.com
A good source for seasonal cookie cutters (we saw 3-D cutters here first) and decorative sugars.

Wilton
800-794-5866
www.wilton.com
A huge selection of their own brand of baking and decorating supplies. We've used many of their products; we've found their prices for cellophane bags to be good.

Zazzle
888-892-9953
www.zazzle.com
We love personalized postage stamps! Put your cookie creations on your envelopes for all the world to see.

index

Pages numbers in *italics* indicate illustrations or photographs; page numbers in **bold** indicate charts